Illicit Trade

E-Commerce Challenges in Illicit Trade in Fakes

GOVERNANCE FRAMEWORKS AND BEST PRACTICES

OECD))
BETTER POLICIES FOR BETTER LIVES

This work is published under the responsibility of the Secretary-General of the OECD. The opinions expressed and arguments employed herein do not necessarily reflect the official views of the Members of the OECD.

This document, as well as any data and map included herein, are without prejudice to the status of or sovereignty over any territory, to the delimitation of international frontiers and boundaries and to the name of any territory, city or area.

Please cite this publication as:
OECD (2021), *E-Commerce Challenges in Illicit Trade in Fakes: Governance Frameworks and Best Practices*, Illicit Trade, OECD Publishing, Paris, *https://doi.org/10.1787/40522de9-en*.

ISBN 978-92-64-88534-9 (print)
ISBN 978-92-64-40744-2 (pdf)

Illicit Trade
ISSN 2617-5827 (print)
ISSN 2617-5835 (online)

Foreword

Trade in counterfeit goods is a longstanding -- and growing -- worldwide socio-economic risk that threatens effective public governance, efficient business, and the well-being of consumers.

One of the areas that have garnered increased attention in recent years has been the use by counterfeiters and other illicit traders of e-commerce to cloak their activities. Trading platforms such as Amazon, eBay have been instrumental in promoting growth in e-commerce, but they can also be abused by illicit trade networks. The COVID-19 pandemic has exacerbated these problems, as people turn to e-commerce during lockdowns and shop closures. Governments and industries have recognised these problems and are addressing them in various ways, including by providing more transparency, streamlining procedures, and facilitating co-operation among e-commerce platforms, right holders and governments.

This study provides an overview of these government- and industry-specific measures to address the abuse of online platforms by counterfeiters. Given the global and borderless nature of e-commerce, such information is crucially needed, not only to better understand this threat and different approaches for tackling it, but also for co-ordinating effective governance responses.

This study was carried out under the auspices of the OECD's Task Force on Countering Illicit Trade, which focuses on evidence-based research and advanced analytics to assist policy makers in mapping and understanding the vulnerabilities exploited by illicit trade.

Acknowledgements

This report was prepared by the OECD Public Governance Directorate (GOV), under the leadership of Elsa Pilichowski, Public Governance Director, and Martin Forst, Head of GOV's Governance Reviews and Partnerships division. It was carried out under the auspices of the Task Force on Countering Illicit Trade (TF-CIT). The study was shared with other OECD committees with relevant expertise in the area of trade, regulatory policy, public sector integrity and digital economy policy.

The report was prepared by Piotr Stryszowski, Senior Economist and Morgane Gaudiau, Economist at the OECD Directorate for Public Governance. Peter Avery and Jean-Paul Rebillard provided significant inputs. The authors wish to thank the OECD experts who provided valuable knowledge and insights: Julio Bacio Terracino, Alessandro Bellantoni and Nick Malyshev from the OECD Public Governance Directorate, and Silvia Sorescu from the OECD Trade Directorate.

The authors would also like to thank experts from the OECD member countries and participants of several seminars and workshops for their valuable assistance. Special expressions of appreciation are given to Henry Bolton from Australian Border Force, Kasie Brill from the US Chamber of Commerce, Juan Cichero from Mercado Libre, Sara Decker from Walmart, Rodney Jeffs from Australian Border Force, prof. Jay Kennedy from Michigan State University, Phil Lewis from the UK Anti-Counterfeiting Group, Robert McNeill from IP Australia, Roland De Meersman from the Belgian Anti-Counterfeiting Association ABAC-BAAN, Angélique Monneraye from DG Grow of the European Commission, Michael Rose from the US National IPR Center, Ashley Shillingsburg from eBay and Mary Beth Westmoreland from Amazon.

Andrea Uhrhammer and Ciara Muller provided editorial and production support.

Table of contents

Follow OECD Publications on:

http://twitter.com/OECD_Pubs

http://www.facebook.com/OECDPublications

http://www.linkedin.com/groups/OECD-Publications-4645871

http://www.youtube.com/oecdilibrary

http://www.oecd.org/oecddirect/

Executive Summary

The Internet has provided new opportunities and mechanisms for trading goods and services via e-commerce. This report analyses the role of e-commerce in the illicit trade in fake goods. In particular, it examines the significant challenges that governments, online platforms, brand owners and consumers are facing with the growing misuse of e-commerce platforms for illicit trade in counterfeit goods.

E-commerce trends and developments

- E-commerce is growing force in economies worldwide. Between 2016 to 2019, business-to-consumer (B2C) online sales rose by 82% to USD 4.2 trillion, with a COVID-19-associated boost of 25.7% in 2020. By 2025, e-commerce retail sales are currently forecast to rise to USD 7.2 trillion, which would represent about 24.5% of total retail sales, as compared to 17.8% in 2020.

- The number of sites engaging in e-commerce is constantly changing, as new players enter the market and others exit. Existing estimates suggest there are currently 12 to 24 million e-commerce sites. Most of them are small. Fewer than one million sellers sell more than USD 1,000 per year. The larger e-commerce companies are multi-billion enterprises, headquartered principally in China and the United States. The 13 largest companies sold goods and services valued at USD 2.9 trillion in 2019, which accounted for close to 60% of total B2C sales in that year.

- E-commerce has given certain distribution channels a big boost, providing a means for businesses to bypass retail outlets and ship small quantities of items directly to individual consumers in a cost-effective way. The distribution channels that have been most favourably affected are the post and local and international express delivery services such as FedEx, UPS and DHL. However, counterfeiters have also successfully exploited these channels. There is little risk of detection, since the quantities of merchandise shipped in individual parcels and letter packets tend to be small and the shipments are intermingled with billions of legitimately traded items. In 2019, some 63.9% of seizures of counterfeit items involved mailed items. Most of the seizures involved a small number of items, with mailed items accounting for only 10% of the total global seized value.

Government actions to combat counterfeiting

In recent years, governments addressed e-commerce fraud in in a variety of ways, by encouraging co-operation with and among stakeholders, and through specific initiatives designed to improve the functioning of e-commerce.

- In Australia, the government is working on a mechanism for consumers to verify authorised sellers of branded products on the seller's website. Consumers would click on a symbol that links to the government's trademark registry, which would in turn authenticate the seller as a supplier of legitimate products.

- In Belgium, the government, in co-operation with law enforcement in other jurisdictions, has focused on policing the Internet, taking down sites trading in counterfeits, in co-operation with law enforcement in other jurisdictions. Considerable attention has been paid to strengthening the registration process for websites; suspicious websites are subject to scrutiny and verification before being authorised.

- In the European Union (EU), the United Kingdom (UK) and the United States (US), working groups were formed to address e-commerce intellectual property (IP) issues. In the EU, a voluntary, non-binding memorandum of understanding (MoU) with rights holders from many industries and platforms was created to tackle problems. The EU Commission, which administers the MoU, plays a supportive role to keep the work on track. In the UK, brand owners have been working with law enforcement to identify websites selling counterfeits. Once claims are vetted, law enforcement provides the information on offending websites to the country's web registrar, which organises the suspension of the websites concerned. In the US, the government formed an Electronic Commerce Working Group (ECWG) under the US Department of Homeland Security (DHS) in 2017 to foster and encourage the flow of actionable data and information between online sales platforms and, ultimately, with shippers, freight forwarders, brokers, and other third-party. In January 2020, the US created the Anti-Counterfeiting Consortium to Identify Online Nefarious Actors (ACTION) to monitor adoption and report on the effectiveness of private sector best practices established in the report on *Combatting Trafficking in Counterfeit and Pirated Goods*.

- Internationally, the European Union Intellectual Property Office (EUIPO) has been working on a webpage providing basic information on the IP protection mechanisms in place on different platforms. As part of the development of its IP Enforcement Portal, it is also developing a system to enable platform operators to identify brand owner contact points in the different areas of IP infringement. There is also interest in developing a secure system that will allow IP owners to report information on infringement, which could then be accessed by participating platform operators.

Actions that platform operators have taken to combat counterfeiting

The major online platforms have developed mechanisms designed to enhance the trust of all parties using their platforms and protect customers, brands, and their stores from counterfeiters. The mechanisms have focused on several action areas, including:

- *Sellers*. Sellers are subject to checks prior to being allowed to trade on online platforms. They are also subject to terms of service agreements that prohibit the sale of counterfeit products and provide the operators with a legal basis to act if counterfeiting is detected.

- *Consumers*. Consumers are provided with tools to easily determine the identity and details of the parties that they are purchasing from, or affirm the authenticity of their purchases through easy-to-use serialization services that protects each individual product unit.

- *Brand rights holders*. Rights holders are provided with tools to screen product listings for counterfeits and ensure that these listings are taken down rapidly.

- *Co-operation among the private-sector and with law enforcement*. Platforms and law enforcement are working together to support legal actions against counterfeiters and share intelligence on developments and trends, in a proactive manner. Some are also proactively sharing information on individuals removed from their platform for allegedly selling counterfeit goods as well as intelligence on developments and trends. Platforms are moving forward with the creation of a private-sector data sharing platform to identify common targets and actionable intelligence about counterfeiters and their criminal networks.

- *Co-operation among private-sector.* Platforms are moving forward with the creation of a private-sector data sharing platform to identify common targets and actionable intelligence about counterfeiters and their criminal networks.
- *Development of internal know-how.* Platforms are developing internal expertise to combat counterfeiting as well as advanced tools that can be used to move proactively against counterfeits. This includes use of heuristics, algorithms and machine learning.
- *Transparency.* Platforms are expanding their reporting on the results of anti-counterfeiting measures through, for example, annual reports on their activities.

Remaining challenges

While stakeholders have taken many actions to combat counterfeiting, significant challenges remain, as criminal networks have been able to react quickly and dynamically to avoid detection and circumvent law enforcement. As a result, governments and industry responses need to be re-examined regularly. In doing so, important issues need to be addressed, including:

- the difficulties in dealing with a vast landscape that includes millions of sellers;
- enforcement gaps and limited institutional capacities exploited by counterfeiters and criminal networks;
- adequately screening cross-border movements of counterfeits, many of which are shipped in small parcels and letter packets; most economies have applied the WTO-TRIPS Article 60 *de minimis* exemption to importations by mail in limited quantities, as opposed to being available only to goods accompanying incoming passengers;
- the flexibility that platform operators need to respond to emerging threats and the role that industry self-regulation could play in responding to emerging challenges;
- the adequacy and effectiveness of national laws, penalties and sanctions to both deter future and hold current counterfeiters accountable through changes to the risk-reward structure for counterfeiting;
- the need for stronger information-sharing and collaboration among public and private stakeholders, both within and across jurisdictions, and involving express delivery carriers, social media, payment processors, and search engines;
- the responsibilities that platform operators should bear in combating counterfeiting activities;
- the need for enhanced scrutiny and vetting of third-party sellers; and
- adequately protecting the privacy of online stakeholders.

Further analysis is needed to support work in the above areas, along with in-depth country studies to enrich the knowledge base and to help identify best practices.

1 E-commerce trends and developments

Background

This report studies the issue of abuse of on-line e-commerce platforms by sellers of counterfeits goods.

The risks of counterfeiting have been analysed by the OECD for more than 10 years. An in-depth report prepared in 2008 analysed the economics underlying the illicit trade, providing sector-specific and country assessments (OECD, 2008[1]). Subsequent work included an assessment of digital piracy (Stryszowski and Scorpecci, 2009[2]) and an analysis of governance frameworks for countering illicit trade (OECD, 2018[3]).

In 2016 the OECD joined forces with the European Union Intellectual Property Office (EUIPO) to deepen the understanding of the scale and magnitude of IP infringement problems in international trade. The results were published in a series of reports that provide a general overview of the situation: *Trade in Counterfeit and Pirated Goods: Mapping the Economic Impact* (OECD/EUIPO, 2016[4]), *Mapping the Real Routes of Trade in Fake Goods* (OECD/EUIPO, 2017[5]) and *Trends in Trade in Counterfeit and Pirated Goods* (OECD/EUIPO, 2019[6]).

In addition to these core reports, further studies have deepened understanding on specific aspects of trade in counterfeit goods. These include *Trade in Counterfeit Goods and Free Trade Zones: Evidence from Recent Trends* (OECD/EUIPO, 2018[7]), *Why Do Countries Export Fakes?: The Role of Governance Frameworks, Enforcement and Socio-economic Factors* (OECD/EUIPO, 2018[8]); *Misuse of Small Parcels for Trade in Counterfeit Goods* (OECD/EUIPO, 2018[9]); *Trade in Counterfeit Pharmaceutical Goods* (OECD/EUIPO, 2020[10]), *Misuse of Containerized Maritime Transport in Counterfeit Trade* (OECD/EUIPO, 2021[11]) and Global Trade in Fakes, A Worrying Threat (OECD/EUIPO, 2021b[12]).

The techniques and strategies of counterfeiters are constantly evolving as they seek to avoid detection. One of the vehicles that they are currently exploiting is e-commerce, which provides expanding opportunities to sell counterfeit products, with a relatively low risk of detection.[1] IP rights holders are deeply concerned about developments and trends and have been working closely with government agencies and e-commerce platforms to address challenges. The stakes are high as growth in business to consumer (B2C) e-commerce sales is soaring globally, rising by 82% between 2016 to 2019, with a COVID-associated boost of 25.7% in 2020, to USD 4.2 trillion.[2] By 2025, e-commerce retail sales are currently forecasted to rise to USD 7.2 trillion, which would represent about 24.5% of total retail sales, as compared to 17.8% in 2020.

This report examines how e-commerce is evolving, identifies some of the key issues and explores what stakeholders are doing to address the challenges posed by counterfeits. The assessments in parts II and III draw extensively on discussions held with the stakeholders through a series of webinars and individual follow-up discussions during April-July 2021.

This report looks at the issue of abuse of online e-commerce platforms by sellers of counterfeits goods. Two important points should be kept in mind in this context:

First, the term "counterfeiting" refers to a range of illicit activities related to the infringement of IP rights mostly trademarks. Following the (OECD, 2008[1]), (OECD/EUIPO, 2016[4]) (OECD/EUIPO, 2019[13]) and (OECD/EUIPO, 2021b[12]) studies, this report focuses primarily on the infringement of copyright, trademarks, design rights and patents The term counterfeit used in this report refers to tangible goods that infringe trademarks, design rights or patents. This wording is used for the purpose of this report only and does not constitute any definition outside its scope. In particular, this study does not include intangible infringements, such as online piracy or infringements of other IPRs. Further, his report does not look at substandard, adulterated or mislabelled products, that do not violate a trademark, patent or design right.

Second, the usage of the term e-commerce varies in different contexts, and the understanding of e-commerce is not universal. For instance, definitions employed by the Eurostat and the US Census Bureau differ with respect to taking into account sales negotiated on extranets, email, and mobile devices (m-commerce). Even though these differences appear slight, one should keep in mind that discussions that fed into this report might come from stakeholders that refer to different definitions of e-commerce. Of course, just as for counterfeiting, this report does not introduce any new definition of e-commerce, rather it uses the working description used in other prior OECD reports[3].

Market trends

The development of the Internet has served buyers and sellers of goods and services well, by greatly enhancing the efficiency of markets, via e-commerce (OECD, 2013[14]). Consumers, for example, can access a broader range of products from a larger number of suppliers, than was previously the case. Additionally, businesses can expand the reach of their operations in a highly cost-effective manner that has proven beneficial to large and smaller entities alike. The increased transparency of markets has at the same time enhanced competition, spurring innovation.

The e-commerce market has three main segments: business to business (B2B), which dominates the market, business to consumer (B2C), which has risen sharply in recent years and consumer to consumer (C2C) which covers the sale of products between individuals that are not treated as businesses.[4] In 2019, e-commerce was estimated at USD 26.7 trillion, which accounted for about 30% of world GDP (Table 1.1). The United States, Japan and China were the top 3 economies in terms of e-commerce sales accounting for close to 60% of the world total. The importance of e-commerce, measured as a share of GDP, varied significantly across economies, ranging from 14% of GDP in the case of Germany, to 79% in the case of Korea (see Table 1.1 for additional measures). As indicated above, B2B transactions dominate the market, accounting for 82% of all e-commerce in 1989, including both sales over online market platforms and electronic data interchange transactions.

Table 1.1. World e-commerce in 2019 (Billions of USD and percent)

Economy	Total e-commerce sales	Share of world total	Share of GDP	B2B e-commerce		B2C e-commerce	
				Sales	% of total sales	Sales	% of total sales
United States	9,580	36	45	8,319	87	1,261	13
Japan	3,416	13	67	3,238	95	178	5
China	2,604	10	18	1,065	41	1,539	59
Korea	1,302	5	79	1,187	91	115	9
United Kingdom	885	3	31	633	72	251	28
France	785	3	29	669	85	116	15
Germany	524	2	14	493	94	111	21
Italy	431	2	22	396	92	35	8

Economy	Total e-commerce sales	Share of world total	Share of GDP	B2B e-commerce		B2C e-commerce	
				Sales	% of total sales	Sales	% of total sales
Australia	347	1	25	325	94	21	6
Spain	344	1	25	280	81	64	19
Subtotal	20,218	76	36	16,526	82	3,691	18
Other	6,455	24	20	5,277	82	1,179	18
Grand total	26,673	100	30	21,803	82	4,870	18

Source: UNCTAD, 2021.

The B2C market has experienced continued and rapid growth in many economies over recent years. Table 1.2 shows how the situation has changed with respect to online retail sales, which represent a subset of the B2C sales reported in Table 1.1. The overall increase in sales of 41% between 2018 and 2020 contrasts with the 0.1% decrease in total retail sales. At the country level, all countries listed experienced growth in online retail sales exceeding 33%, with sales in Canada and Singapore doubling. Total retail sales, on the other hand, declined in five of the seven economies listed, rising by less than 2% in the remaining two. As a result, the share of online retail sales to the total rose sharply in all the economies, increasing to more than 20% in three economies.

Table 1.2. Retail sales in selected economies, 2018-20 (Billions of USD and percent)

Economy	Online retail sales			Total retail sales			Online share of total		
	2018	2019	2020	2018	2019	2020	2018	2019	2020
Australia	13.5	14.4	22.9	239	229	242	5.6	6.3	9.4
Canada	13.9	16.5	28.1	467	462	452	3.0	3.6	6.2
China	1,060.4	1,233.6	1,414.3	5,755	5,957	5,681	18.4	20.7	24.9
Korea	76.8	84.3	104.4	423	406	403	18.2	20.8	25.9
Singapore	1.6	1.9	3.2	34	32	27	4.7	5.9	11.7
United Kingdom	84.0	89.0	130.6	565	564	560	14.9	15.8	23.3
United States	519.6	598.0	791.7	5,269	5,452	5,368	9.9	11.0	14.0
Total of above	1,770	2,038	2,495	12,752	13,102	12,773	14	16	19

Source: UNCTAD, 2021.

The recent rise in online activity is, however, part of a longer-term trend. In the United States, for example, B2C e-commerce shipments rose by 267% during 2008-18, compared to 85% in the case of B2B manufacturing shipments.[5] In the process, the share of e-commerce retail sales to the total rose from 3.6% in 2008 to 9.9% in 2018, and to as high as 15.2% in the fourth quarter of 2020; at the same time the share of B2B manufacturing online activity rose from 40% in 2008, to 67% in 2018. Moreover, in the United Kingdom, B2C retail sales surged during 2020 and into 2021, jumping from 4.9% in 2008, to 28% in 2020 and 33% during January-April 2021.[6]. By the end of 2021, some 93% of UK Internet users are expected to have engaged in e-commerce (OECD, 2021[15]). Surveys indicate that the shift to online purchases is likely to continue as some 60% of those surveyed expected their online purchases to continue at elevated levels following the pandemic.

The Internet provides an effective mechanism for engaging in B2C cross-border trade, which in 2019 amounted to USD 440 billion (UNCTAD, 2021[16]). As shown in Table 1.3, cross border transactions represented 2.3% of world merchandise exports in that year. While their role was relatively small in some economies, it reached 8.2% in the case of the United Kingdom. The share of cross border transactions in total B2C transactions amounted to 9%, exceeding 10% in six of the top 10 merchandise exporters listed.

Table 1.3. Cross-border B2C e-commerce sales of the top 10 merchandise exporters, 2019 (Billions of USD and percent)

Economy	Sales	Share of total merchandise exports	Share of total B2C e-commerce sales
China	105	4.2	6.8
United States	90	5.5	7.1
United Kingdom	38	8.2	15.2
Hong Kong, China	35	6.2	94.3
Japan	23	3.3	13.2
Germany	16	1.1	14.7
France	12	2.2	10.6
Korea	5	0.9	4.4
Italy	5	0.9	13.9
Netherlands	1	0.2	4.3
Total of above	332	3.4	9.0
World	440	2.3	9.0

Source: UNCTAD, 2021.

Industry structure

Overview

Goods and services can be sold on the Internet via e-commerce by companies, organisations and individuals, regardless of their size. Individuals, for example, can set up store fronts easily, at low cost, as can small shops. The number of sites engaging in e-commerce is constantly changing as new players enter the market and others exit. Some have estimated that there are currently 12 to 24 million e-commerce sites; most are small as less than one million sellers sell more than USD 1,000 per year.[7] The larger e-commerce companies are multi-billion enterprises, headquartered principally in China and the United States (Table 1.4). The 13 largest e-commerce companies sold goods and services valued at USD 2.9 trillion in 2019, which accounted for close to 60% of total B2C sales in that year.

Table 1.4. Largest B2C e-commerce companies, 2020 (Billions of USD)

Company	Headquarters	Gross merchandise volume		
		2018	2019	2020
Alibaba	China	866	954	1,145
Amazon	United States	344	417	575
JD.com	China	253	302	379
Pinduoduo	China	71	146	242
Shopify	Canada	41	61	120
eBay	United States	90	86	100
Meituan	China	43	57	71
Walmart	United States	25	37	64
Uber	United States	50	65	58
Rakuten	Japan	30	34	42
Expedia	United States	100	108	37

Company	Headquarters	Gross merchandise volume		
		2018	**2019**	**2020**
Booking Holdings	United States	93	96	35
Airbnb	United States	29	38	24
Total	--	2,035	2,401	2,892

Source: UNCTAD, 2021.

As indicated above, there are various types of B2C e-commerce platforms. *Marketplace platforms*, such as Alibaba, Amazon and eBay, sell a broad range of products, which are offered for sale from internal stocks or by outside vendors. The platform operator is responsible for attracting potential customers, advertising offers and processing transactions; they may also take responsibility for shipping products to buyers. *Retail store platforms* are operated by brick-and-mortar businesses; they provide consumers with a means to shop for and purchase products, for pick-up or shipping. They may also offer products from third party vendors, serving, in this case, as a marketplace platform as well. Other types of platforms include those operated by companies that offer virtual products or services, and those operated by manufacturers interested in selling their branded products directly to consumers, such as Apple, Godiva, Gucci, Levi's, Tiffany and Nike.

In terms of trends, conventional firms and retailers are increasingly experimenting with online distribution channels, alongside their brick-and-mortar operations (OECD, 2020[17]). This includes smaller retailers that are trying to survive due to the drop-off of sales in physical stores during the pandemic. There are challenges however as leveraging the Internet, or other electronic networks, to integrate e-commerce into an existing firm-level business model often requires complementary investments. These can include supply-chain and fulfilment arrangements, as well as consolidated inventory systems. In general, however, e-commerce shows much promise for small and medium enterprises (SMEs), provided they have the resources needed to establish and maintain their own websites or, alternatively, engage with e-commerce platforms. There is scope for significant expansion; in 2019, e-commerce accounted for 24% of economic turnover in large firms, but only 10% in small firms (OECD, 2020[17]).

Innovation is ongoing in e-commerce markets. Sellers have, for example, deployed "click-and-collect" mechanisms, which enable consumers to order and purchase online and then collect purchased items in a local brick-and-mortar store or another location, such as a locker (OECD, 2020[17]). This allows consumers to immediately purchase a good or service at a distance, and to save on shipping costs, delays and the inconveniences that may be associated with delivery. The "click-and-collect" mechanism enables firms to retain their centralized inventory system, while reducing the operational costs associated with physical brick-and-mortar stores. Furthermore, it enables them to acquire useful data about users. To the extent that click-and-collect mechanisms are in a brick-and-mortar store, they may allow consumers to check the quality and assess the colour, style and size of a product within the store itself prior to purchase. In addition, consumers can often make returns in-store, which can increase their willingness to purchase online.

Some online businesses in the apparel sectors are innovating by including offline features to enable the sale of fit-critical goods and services online (OECD, 2020[17]). While an offline distribution channel may increase costs, it can increase the extensive margin of e-commerce by enabling new types of products to be sold online. Firms that sell heterogeneous or customized products like clothing may benefit from consumers' ability to physically inspect the product before purchase. For example, several online apparel retailers have opened brick-and-mortar stores that allow consumers to try on products before ordering them online.

Other firms are experimenting with online ordering mechanisms within or near brick-and-mortar stores (OECD, 2020[17]). After entering a store via a mobile application, consumers can select the products and then leave the store without a formal checkout.

Distribution

E-commerce has given certain distribution channels a big boost, providing a means for businesses to bypass retail outlets and ship small quantities of items directly to individual consumers in a cost-effective manner. The success of this business strategy is borne out by the profitability and growth of the largest e-commerce market platforms. The distribution channels that have been most favourably affected are the postal services and local and international express delivery services such as FedEx, UPS and DHL. In the case of the post, traffic in domestic and international letters has declined sharply over time, falling by close to one third from 2001 to 2019 (Table 1.5). On the other hand, fuelled by e-commerce, the volume of parcel traffic, both domestic and international more than quadrupled during the same time, rising to 21.3 billion items in 2019.[8] In the five-year period 2015-2019 alone, parcel traffic rose by more than 70%.

Table 1.5. Processing of letters and parcels by postal authorities in recent years

Year	Letters			Parcels		
	Domestic	International	Total	Domestic	International	Total
	Billions				Millions	Billions
2001	416	6.9	423	4.8	43	4.8
2010	356	4.3	360	8.0	62	8.1
2015	310	3.3	313	12.2	115	12.3
2016	301	3.1	304	14.6	133	14.7
2017	303	2.9	306	16.3	174	16.5
2018	290	2.7	293	18.4	179	18.6
2019	284	2.6	287	21.1	192	21.3

Source: UPU (see https://www.upu.int/en/Universal-Postal-Union/Activities/Research-Publications/Postal-Statistics#query-the-database, accessed 18 July 2021.

While statistics are not yet available for 2020 and 2021, the impact of COVID-19 could well have accelerated the growth in parcel trade. In the United States, for example, mail volumes declined precipitously in FY2020[9] as marketers restrained from spending and adapted to changes in consumer behaviour (USPS, 2020/21[18])). Package volumes, on the other hand, rose by 19% from FY2019 to FY2020, to 7.3 billion pieces as people minimized in-person shopping and ordered goods delivered to their homes.

Postal services are keen on strengthening their participation in e-commerce. The United States Postal Service (USPS), for example, has focused on growing e-commerce and implementing marketing campaigns to increase business by offering day-specific delivery, improved tracking, text alerts and up to USD 100 of free insurance included on most Priority Mail packages. At the international level, the Universal Postal Union (UPU) updated its e-commerce guide (originally published in 2014), in 2020, to include new and expanded information on recent trends, business models, e-commerce key elements, strategies and UPU enablers to facilitate e-commerce (UPU, 2020[19]).

As noted, the ability of suppliers to furnish consumers with goods in a cost-effective manner via the post and related delivery services has been highly beneficial for the parties concerned. It has, however, provided an opening for those involved in illicit trade to carry out their operations with little risk of detection as the quantities of merchandise shipped in individual parcels and letter packets tend to be small and the shipments are intermingled with billions of legitimately traded items. Additionally, the law of the vast majority of economies exempts importations in small quantities from being subject to seizure for infringing intellectual property rights, whereas a minority of economies have only exempted from seizure small quantities of infringing items that accompany an incoming passenger, are for their personal use only, and are not packaged for retail sale.

The problem is a significant one that commands considerable attention from legislative and enforcement authorities. In the case of items that cross borders, the OECD estimated that counterfeits amounted to USD 503 billion in 2016, or 3.3% of world trade; the problem, it was noted, is growing worse.[10] Trade in counterfeits via parcels is an important vehicle for facilitating the illicit trade, which is reflected in seizures by border officials. In 2019, some 63.9% of seizures involved mailed items (WCO, 2020). Most of the seizures involved a small number of items, with mail accounting for only 12.1% of the total number of items seized.[11] The challenges in combatting the counterfeits are ongoing as the criminal networks involved are constantly adapting their techniques to evade the efforts of enforcement authorities to intercept the illicit products (OECD/EUIPO, 2020[10]). Problems are seen as most pronounced in goods moving through postal channels, given the difficulties in screening the huge volume of small parcels and letter packets moving within and across borders and the limited or misleading information that can be provided on the content of parcels and packets (OECD, 2021[15]).

E-commerce fraud

One of the top concerns about e-commerce is its potential to be used to commit fraud. This reflects the ease with which purveyors of counterfeit, pirated goods and/or unsafe goods can pollute e-commerce distribution channels. Selling counterfeit and pirated merchandise is illegal as it infringes trademark and copyright law, to the detriment of the companies which developed the goods concerned. Counterfeit products often do not meet regulatory standards that legitimate goods must. Unsafe products consists of all goods which threaten consumer health and safety, whether or not they infringe intellectual property rights. As discussed below, the largest marketplace platform providers have developed mechanisms to undermine the bad actors who, knowingly or unknowingly, seek to sell illicit or unsafe goods via e-commerce. Governments have also taken measures in this regard, but the challenges are great and remain of keen concern to all stakeholders, with some governments now actively pursuing legislation to address problems.

As mentioned above, it is relatively easy to set up e-commerce websites in most jurisdictions, as the large number (12 to 24 million) attests. Fraudsters who are intent on swindling consumers are thus in good position to establish a web presence, through which their fraudulent acts can be committed. Many of the fraudsters who establish sites are active traders of counterfeit and pirated products. Once detected, governments can act to have rogue websites taken down; the ease of re-establishing such websites using new domain names, however, is problematic.

In addition to national actions, several initiatives have been taken at the international level to combat the online sale of counterfeit items. INTERPOL, for example, has coordinated campaigns against the online sale of illicit drugs and medical devices (OECD/EUIPO, 2020[10]). Operation Pangea has been carried out since 2008, with the number of countries participating rising from 8 to a record 123 in 2017. Participating agencies carried out coordinated operational activities against illegal websites during the same week with a view towards identifying the criminal networks behind the trafficking (Table 1.6). During Pangea XI, which was carried out in 2018, police, customs and health regulatory authorities from 116 countries targeted the illicit online sale of medicines and medical products, resulting in 859 arrests worldwide and the seizure of USD 14 million worth of potentially dangerous pharmaceuticals. Almost one million packages were inspected during the week of action, with 500 tonnes of illicit pharmaceuticals seized worldwide. Seizures included anti-inflammatory medication, painkillers, erectile dysfunction pills, hypnotic and sedative agents, anabolic steroids, slimming pills and medicines for treating HIV, Parkinson's and diabetes. More than 110,000 medical devices including syringes, contact lenses, hearing aids and surgical instruments were also seized.

Table 1.6. Operation Pangea 2008-2018

Year (Pangea number)	Number of countries	Seizures		Number of arrests	Number of websites closed
		Quantity	Value (millions of USD)		
2008 (I)	10	NA	NA	NA	NA
2009 (II)	24	167,000 items	NA	22[1]	72
2010 (III)	45	1 million	2.6	NA	290
2011 (IV)	81	2.4 million items	6.3	55[1]	13,500
2012 (V)	100	3.75 million items	10.5	80	18,000
2013 (VI)	100	9.8 million items	41	58	9,000
2014 (VII)	111	9.4 million items	31	237	10,600
2015 (VIII)	115	20.7 million items	81	156	2,414
2016 (IX)	103	12.2 million items	53	393	4,932
2017 (X)	123	25 million items	51	400	3,584
2018 (XI)	116	500 tones	14	859	3,671

Notes: [1] Arrested or under investigation; 2 NA: Not available

Source: INTERPOL news releases at www.interpol.int/News-and-Events.

One of the main trends identified during the decade of Pangea operations is the continuous growth of unauthorised and unregulated online pharmacies, which are capitalising on increasing consumer demand worldwide.[12] Also of note, criminals are shipping packages containing smaller numbers of pills and tablets to try and avoid the more stringent checks which have become routine in many countries.[13]

Social media

Use in e-commerce

Another trend concerns the emergence of social media platforms as vehicles for facilitating e-commerce.[14] Businesses have become active on the platforms, which are being used by them to deepen interactions with consumers. Social networks, which are the most popular online activity in most countries, were used by nearly three-quarters of Internet users in the OECD in 2019 (OECD, 2020[17]). Businesses have taken note; more than half in the OECD had a social media presence in 2017, up from one-third in 2013. As in other areas, there is a marked contrast between countries. Usage ranged from over 65% in Iceland, Norway, Brazil, the Netherlands, Ireland and Denmark, to below 30% in Japan, Poland and Mexico. Medium and large enterprises are the predominant users. In 2017, less than one in three small firms in the OECD used social media compared to almost three-quarters of large firms. Growth in e-commerce, combined with similar growth in social media usage has encouraged companies to turn to influencer marketing (see below) and user generated content to promote brand awareness (Phaneuf, 2021[20]).

Businesses primarily use social media for developing the enterprise's image and marketing products, as well as to obtain or respond to customer opinions, reviews or questions (OECD, 2020[17]). They may also use social media to involve customers in the development or innovation of goods or services. The use of social media for commercial purposes (referred to as "social commerce") is booming, with US retail social commerce sales forecast to rise by 34.8% in 2021, to $36.1 billion, representing 4.3% of all retail e-commerce sales (Phaneuf, 2021[20]). While fashion categories including apparel and accessories are the largest segment of social commerce, electronics and home decor are also significant. Companies can use influencers, consumer call to actions, and user generated content, to capitalize on the power of social commerce.

Influencers

One aspect of note is the role of "influencers" on social media platforms. Influencers are persons who can generate interest in something (such as a consumer product) by posting on social media (AAFA, 2021[21]). Once limited to celebrities with massive followings, influencers now include a growing number of persons with more limited followings, who nonetheless can have significant impact on the sales of a product. Influencers are in fact considered to be a vital part of the fashion industry, with many brands incorporating influencer marketing into their digital strategies. The brands count on the influencers to promote their brands in ways that complement their traditional marketing strategies. The influencer industry is large and growing, with estimates that it will be worth $15 billion by 2022.

Influencers can thus play a critical role when it comes to shopping decisions online (AAFA, 2021[21]). People who follow influencers tend to consider them more as friends or acquaintances, rather than celebrities or advertisers. The influencers can therefore help to build trust and authentic relationships with followers, with their recommendations having considerable weight in consumer decisions.

With respect to counterfeiting, concern has been expressed about the growth of "dupe" influencers, which are persons who use their influence to promote off brand or, in some cases, counterfeit items. In some instances these influencers claim or suggest that the items are genuine, or just like a similar branded product. In the past, the counterfeit products have been referred to as "knockoffs," "reps," "AAA," "mirror quality," "replicas," and "inspired" (AAFA, 2021[21]). In recent times, the term "dupes" has gained popularity on social media platforms to refer to counterfeits. Some dupe influencers pride themselves as providing online resources for finding fake versions of highly sought-after fashion items.

The tactics used by the influencers include i) unboxing promotional videos, ii) sponsorships and giveaways, iii) tutorial videos and hidden links, and iv) influencer shopping apps (AAFA, 2021[21]). The influencers use the *unboxing videos* to showcase their products. The unboxing videos typically start with commentary on where the item was purchased and/or gifted from, how much it cost, and how long it took for the product to arrive. Typically, dupe influencers will film the process of unwrapping or unboxing the product, along with their reaction. The influencers will then comment on the quality of the product, sometimes posting side by side comparisons of the authentic and the counterfeit or go into a detailed analysis of what makes the two versions different. The influencers can also act as *sponsors* for suppliers of counterfeit products, receiving free merchandise for review; influencer followers may also be provided with special discount codes to encourage sales. Additional free merchandise may be provided to the influencer, with a view towards promoting the products through giveaways. *Tutorial videos* posted by influencers include specific, step-by-step tips and tricks to find popular counterfeit items. *Influencer shopping apps* have streamlined the process to shop for counterfeits. Dupe influencers will often direct their social media followers to their tagged posts on these apps.

In some instances the influencers promoting a counterfeit provide links to nondescript or generic products which are being sold on online shopping platforms; the actual product being sold, however, is the counterfeit (OECD discussions, 2021). This technique is designed to undermine the efforts of rights holders and platforms to detect and remove listings for counterfeit products.

COVID-19

The COVID-19 pandemic has re-shaped illicit trade in counterfeit goods. Regarding the observed effects, enforcement officials highlight that the pandemic has aggravated existing problems, through lockdowns, closed borders, and closures of shops.

Criminal networks have reacted very quickly to the crisis, by taking advantage of people working online at home, with less secure infrastructure. Law enforcement officials have reported significant growth in cybercrime, including fraud and phishing. According to law enforcement authorities, in the EU, e-commerce is a predominant channel for distributing fraudulent COVID-19 related products.

The boom of misuse of the online environment also resulted in a considerable growth of abuse of online marketplace and online platforms that were created during the COVID-crisis. Apart from websites, criminals are also beginning to misuse new online channels of communication, such as WhatsApp and Facebook messenger.

Enforcement and industry experts report observable growth in the online supply of counterfeit goods that occurs on all types of online platforms, including those that used to be relatively free from this risk. In addition, a large number of new platforms and domains have been created with the purpose of deceiving consumers. For example, since March 2020, at least 100 000 new domain names containing COVID-19 related words (e.g. Covid, corona or virus) were registered to sell related medical items. This also reflects growing demand for pharmaceuticals and personal protective equipment (PPE) such as masks, safety glasses, protective clothing. Counterfeiters exploit this demand by offering online fake PPEs and counterfeit equipment to produce the PPEs or spare parts of machines.

Online platforms tend to be aware of these risks. For example, during the pandemic, Amazon detected price gouging and ill-described (including counterfeit) goods. Amazon reacted quickly and has worked closely with legal and communication teams, and collaborated with EU law enforcement to share information related to fraudulent goods related to COVID-19 pandemics.

Consumers

Developments and trends

Internet use, of which e-commerce is but one aspect, has risen sharply (OECD, 2020[17]). In 2019, 70% to 95% of adults used the Internet in OECD countries with smartphones became the favoured device for Internet access. There are, however, disparities within age groups and education level. Some 58% of individuals aged 55-74 used the Internet frequently in 2019, which is up from 30% in 2010. On the other hand, nearly 95% of individuals aged 16-24 were daily Internet users.

Increased Internet use is also reflected in an expanding number of persons engaging in B2C e-commerce. In 2019, some 1.48 billion persons, or close to one quarter of the world's population aged 15 and older, made purchases online (Table 1.7) (UNCTAD, 2021[16]). This represented a 16.5% increase over the 1.27 billion e-consumers in 2017. While consumers bought mostly from domestic vendors, some 360 million made cross-border purchases, a 38.4% increase form 2017. As a result, the share of persons making cross-border purchases rose from 20% in 2017, to 25% in 2019.

Table 1.7. Number of online shoppers worldwide, 2017-19

Type of purchase	2017	2018	2019
Cross-border	0.26	0.29	0.36
Domestic	1.01	1.09	1.12
Total	1.27	1.38	1.48

Source: UNCTAD, 2021.

In the OECD area, B2C e-commerce was more pronounced. Almost 60% of individuals bought products online in 2019, up from 38% in 2010 (OECD, 2020[17]). Within the area, the share of people buying online still varied significantly across countries, as well as across different product categories. Age, education, income and experience all influenced uptake. In Denmark, the Netherlands and the United Kingdom, more than 80% of adults shopped online, while in other countries, the participation level was 25%, or less. In 2018, the items most purchased online were clothing, footwear and sporting goods, and travel products, event tickets, reading materials, movies and music, photographic, telecommunication and optical equipment, and food and grocery products. The trend towards online shopping is expected to continue, especially considering the COVID-19 pandemic, with an ever-increasing number of persons buying products using mobile devices (OECD, 2020[17]). In addition to purchasing items, consumers are also increasingly selling goods and services online. In 2019, nearly 20% of individuals in the European Union sold goods or services online, which was more than double the 2008 level.

With respect to trends, subscription services provided through e-commerce channels are becoming more popular (OECD, 2020[17]). Such subscriptions are characterized by regular and recurring payments for the repeated provision of a good or service. In the e-commerce context, this can include subscription to streaming digital products, such as movies, as well as subscriptions to products, such as food or cosmetics which deplete with use and require replenishment. Online technologies enable easy ordering of the goods and services, avoiding associated transaction costs and thus improving convenience for consumers. Firms, on the other hand, benefit from regular and ongoing revenue streams. Interestingly, connected devices that use streams of data through sensors, software and network connections have become linked with physical goods to make continuous or recurring purchases.

Counterfeits

As suggested above, the counterfeit market targets different types of consumers: i) those who will buy counterfeits thinking that the product they are purchasing is genuine, ii) those who knowingly purchase lower-priced counterfeits, and iii) those who do not know whether a product is genuine or counterfeit, and do not care. Persons who knowingly purchase counterfeits or are indifferent may expose themselves to health and safety risks if the counterfeits are substandard. The consequences of buying the counterfeit may be low, or, in the case of food, drugs and electrical equipment the consequences could life-threatening; in these cases consumers are likely to be selective in the types of potentially counterfeit products that they would buy.

Raising consumer awareness of the risks and potential consequences of purchasing counterfeits, including the potential enrichment of organised crime groups which are involved in counterfeiting and the damaging environmental impact of counterfeits, is viewed as a necessary element of anti-counterfeiting strategies by stakeholders (OECD, 2021[15]). Such programmes can provide concerned consumers with information on how to detect and avoid counterfeits, and hopefully can have positive effects on longer term perceptions on the value of IP protection, to rights holders and the economy at large. At the same time, the limited impact of such campaigns on persons who seek out counterfeits requires that other actions are needed to disrupt counterfeit markets.

The quantitative analysis provided in OECD-EUIPO (2021) sheds more light on the quantitative relationship between illicit trade in counterfeits and the indicators on e-commerce. Findings confirm a positive and statistically significant correlation between the indicators of e-commerce activity in an economy, and imports of counterfeits to that economy.

Furthermore, the correlation becomes stronger for indicators of imports of fakes with small parcels. Countries that report high degrees of e-commerce intensity tend to report higher rates of imports of fakes smuggled in small parcels. Although indirectly, it shows that small parcels tend to be the preferred way of shipping of fake products ordered via e-commerce. A closer look into specific streams reveals that the postal distribution channel clearly dominates. Over 90% of seizures of fakes ordered online were carried by post.

In terms of products, many types of fake products tend to be ordered on-line including footwear, clothes, toys, leather goods, electric equipment and watches and cosmetics (Figure 1.1). Looking at the values of seizures, instead of their numbers, yields similar results, with footwear and clothing being product categories on top of the list of products with highest shares of detentions.

Figure 1.1. Distribution of number of detentions not related to online sales between product categories

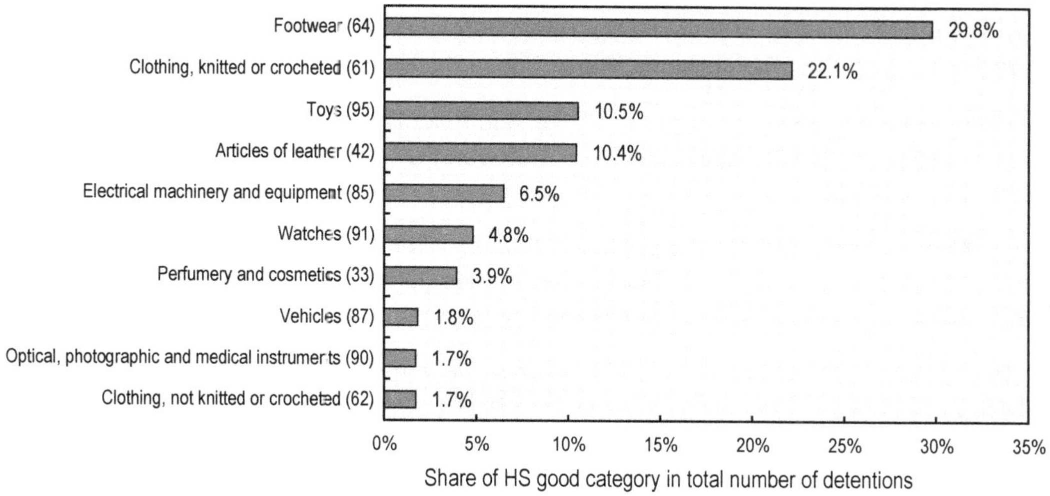

Source: OECD-EUIPO, 2021.

References

AAFA (2021), *Dupe Influencers: The Concerning Trend of Promoting Counterfeit Apparel, Footwear, and Accessories on Social Media*, American Apparel & Footwear Association, http://www.aafaglobal.org/AAFA/Solutions_Pages/Dupe_Influencers_The_Concerning_Trend_of_Prom. [21]

OECD (2021), *Discussions with stakeholders*, unpublished. [15]

OECD (2020), *OECD Digital Economy Outlook 2020*, OECD Publishing, Paris, https://dx.doi.org/10.1787/bb167041-en. [17]

OECD (2018), *Governance Frameworks to Counter Illicit Trade*, Illicit Trade, OECD Publishing, Paris, https://dx.doi.org/10.1787/9789264291652-en. [3]

OECD (2013), "Electronic and Mobile Commerce", *OECD Digital Economy Papers*, No. 228, OECD Publishing, Paris, https://dx.doi.org/10.1787/5k437p2gxw6g-en. [14]

OECD (2008), *The Economic Impact of Counterfeiting and Piracy*, OECD Publishing, Paris, https://dx.doi.org/10.1787/9789264045521-en. [1]

OECD/EUIPO (2021), *Misuse of Containerized Maritime Shipping in the Global Trade of Counterfeits*, Illicit Trade, OECD Publishing, Paris, https://dx.doi.org/10.1787/e39d8939-en. [11]

OECD/EUIPO (2020), *Trade in Counterfeit Pharmaceutical Products*, Illicit Trade, OECD Publishing, Paris, https://dx.doi.org/10.1787/a7c7e054-en. [10]

OECD/EUIPO (2019), *Trends in Trade in Counterfeit and Pirated Goods*, Illicit Trade, OECD Publishing, Paris/European Union Intellectual Property Office, Alicante, https://dx.doi.org/10.1787/g2g9f533-en. [13]

OECD/EUIPO (2019), *Trends in Trade in Counterfeit and Pirated Goods*, Illicit Trade, OECD [6]
Publishing, Paris/European Union Intellectual Property Office, Alicante,
https://dx.doi.org/10.1787/g2g9f533-en.

OECD/EUIPO (2018), *Misuse of Small Parcels for Trade in Counterfeit Goods: Facts and* [9]
Trends, Illicit Trade, OECD Publishing, Paris, https://dx.doi.org/10.1787/9789264307858-en.

OECD/EUIPO (2018), *Trade in Counterfeit Goods and Free Trade Zones: Evidence from Recent* [7]
Trends, Illicit Trade, OECD Publishing, Paris/European Union Intellectual Property Office,
Alicante, https://dx.doi.org/10.1787/9789264289550-en.

OECD/EUIPO (2018), *Why Do Countries Export Fakes?: The Role of Governance Frameworks,* [8]
Enforcement and Socio-economic Factors, Illicit Trade, OECD Publishing, Paris/European
Union Intellectual Property Office, Alicante, https://dx.doi.org/10.1787/9789264302464-en.

OECD/EUIPO (2017), *Mapping the Real Routes of Trade in Fake Goods*, Illicit Trade, OECD [5]
Publishing, Paris, https://dx.doi.org/10.1787/9789264278349-en.

OECD/EUIPO (2016), *Trade in Counterfeit and Pirated Goods: Mapping the Economic Impact*, [4]
Illicit Trade, OECD Publishing, Paris, https://dx.doi.org/10.1787/9789264252653-en.

OECD/EUIPO (2021b), *Global Trade in Fakes: a Worrying Threat*, OECD Publishing, [12]
https://www.oecd.org/publications/global-trade-in-fakes-74c81154-en.htm.

Phaneuf, A. (2021), *Social Commerce 2021: Social media and Ecommerce Convergence Trends* [20]
Brings Growth Opportunity for Brands, Insider Inc., http://www.businessinsider.com/social-
commerce-brand-trends-marketing-strategies.

Stryszowski, P. and D. Scorpecci (2009), *Piracy of Digital Content*, OECD Publishing, Paris, [2]
https://dx.doi.org/10.1787/9789264065437-en.

UNCTAD (2021), *Estimates of global e-commerce 2019 and preliminary assessment of COVID-* [16]
19 impact on online retail 2020, United Nations Conference on Trade and Development,
Geneva, https://unctad.org/system/files/official-document/tn_unctad_ict4d18_en.pd.

UPU (2020), *E-commerce Guide*, Universal Postal Union, Berne, [19]
https://www.upu.int/UPU/media/upu/publications/Final-November-update-UPU-E-Commerce-
Guide_2020_EN.pdf.

USPS (2020/21), *FY 2020 Annual Report to Congress*, United States Postal Service, [18]
https://about.usps.com/what/financials/annual-reports/fy2020.pdf.

Notes

[1]   The OECD defines e-commerce transactions as those involving the sale or purchase of goods or services, conducted over computer networks by methods specifically designed for the purpose of receiving or placing of orders. The goods or services are ordered by those methods, but the payment and the ultimate delivery of the goods or services do not have to be conducted online. An e-commerce transaction can be between enterprises, households, individuals, governments, and other public or private organisations. To be included are orders made over the web, extranet or electronic data interchange. The type is defined by the method of placing the order. To be excluded are orders made by telephone calls, facsimile or manually typed e-mail. (See https://stats.oecd.org/glossary/detail.asp?ID=4721.

[2]   See www.statista.com/statistics/379046/worldwide-retail-e-commerce-sales/ and www.emarketer.com/content/global-ecommerce-forecast-2021.

[3]   See https://www.oecd-ilibrary.org/sites/1885800a-en/index.html?itemId=/content/component/1885800a-en

[4]   Other segments include consumer to business (C2B), consumer to government and (C2G) and business to government (B2G).

[5]   See www.census.gov/retail/index.html.

[6]   See www.ons.gov.uk/businessindustryandtrade/retailindustry/timeseries/j4mc/drsi .

[7]   See https://wpforms.com/ecommerce-statistics/.

[8]   The data on parcels does not include the considerable number of items that are sent in letter packets, data on which are not readily available.

[9]   The year ending on 30 September 2020.

[10]   See https://www.oecd.org/newsroom/trade-in-fake-goods-is-now-33-of-world-trade-and-rising.htm.

[11]   The number of seaborne seizures was far lower, but the number of items seized was considerably higher as the counterfeits tend to be shipped in bulk.

[12]   See www.europol.europa.eu/newsroom/news/millions-of-medicines-seized-in-largest-operation-against-illicit-online-pharmacies.

[13]   See www.interpol.int/en/News-and-Events/News/2018/Illicit-online-pharmaceuticals-500-tonnes-seized-in-global-operation.

[14]   Facebook, Instagram, Pinterest, TikTok and WeChat are examples of social media platforms.

2 Issues

Governments, platform operators and brand rights holders have actively pursued mechanisms to combat counterfeiting and piracy in e-commerce. Some of these are described Part III of this report. Despite the actions that have been taken, counterfeiting remains a significant problem, which many believe is getting worse as counterfeiters find new and innovative ways to expand their sales. Following are some of the issues that were raised in the discussions carried out with stakeholders in recent webinars and follow-up discussions with experts.

Flexibility

In dealing with emerging challenges, several stakeholders have stressed the importance of providing the platform operators with flexibility so that they will be in position to innovate and adapt their technologies and processes to counter the evolving activities of bad actors. Approaches would likely differ among operators, given their different business strategies and situations.

Rights holders noted that the lack of uniform approaches among platforms, while understandable, was nonetheless burdensome, particularly with regards to the anti-counterfeiting mechanisms available to them. It was hoped that the situation could, in general, be simplified and somewhat standardized at least with regards to vetting third-party sellers, disclosures and take downs, and that the burdens placed on rights holders could be lightened.

Collaboration

There is general agreement among stakeholders that collaboration is key to combatting counterfeiting successfully. Much has in fact been achieved in this regard and efforts to expand the collaboration are promising. However, the extent to which it expands may be limited by legal constraints, and private business may be reluctant for various reasons to engage in such voluntary collaboration and information sharing. Efforts to overcome such obstacles need to be considered and pursued.

Such collaboration is critical for developing improved techniques for unravelling and dismantling rings of counterfeiters and dealing with repeat offenders. The counterfeiting rings are usually not acting alone, and they are not focused on a single platform; collaboration could be used to address problems more effectively through co-ordinated, collective efforts. In this regard, it was suggested that it would be helpful if platforms could find a way to share at least some information provided to law enforcement in cases involving confirmed counterfeiters more broadly. There is also potential for the industry to start helping identify trends. During the COVID-19 pandemic, for example, there were shifts in counterfeiting activities, and sharing knowledge between stakeholders would have benefitted governments as well as the platform community.

In setting up collaborative mechanisms, it was suggested that careful attention needs to be paid to the goals of the mechanism. To be successful collaboration would need to be proactive, candid and consistent.

If the participation of some stakeholders inhibited the process, consideration should be given to modifying by setting up different groups.

It was noted that leveraging partnerships with financial intermediaries may be of significant value in enhancing the ways that counterfeiting challenges are addressed, given the underlying mercenary nature of counterfeiting activities. Initiatives that are being taken in this area need to be continued and strengthened.

In addition, given the need for proactive responses to emerging counterfeiting challenges, and the need for speed in addressing these challenges, it was suggested that industry self-regulation could play an important role in developing fluid, timely responses. This might be facilitated by giving an industry body administrative, rulemaking and enforcement authority. Traditional government regulation is viewed as too reactive and slow to address problems, given the speed with which counterfeiters adapt to regulation and their noteworthy abilities to identify and exploit weaknesses in anti-counterfeiting measures.

With respect to international co-operation and collaboration, it was noted that increased information sharing among countries and companies on the actions that they are taking to combat counterfeiting and piracy would be beneficial and contribute importantly to the development of best practices.

Diverse landscape

The platform landscape is diverse, populated by the major, large platforms and many smaller ones. Most attention is focused on the larger ones, given their impact and the limited resources available to move against counterfeits. Learning about effective practices from the larger platforms may, however, have value for the smaller platforms as they develop their strategies for combatting counterfeiting.

Strong measures are needed across the board as bad actors will naturally explore ways to overcome obstacles to their illicit trade by exploiting weaknesses. In this regard, the landscape is continuing to evolve, with the emergence of social media raising new issues with respect to ecommerce; it is an area that counterfeiters are actively exploiting, which is of great concern. Another area requiring attention is the activities of the "dark web", which could be used to exchange information which is then used to facilitate offline trade in counterfeit goods. The role of rogue registrars and registries also deserves attention.

Liability

With respect to platform liability, increased attention to the criteria that could be established for platforms to achieve "safe harbour" status would be beneficial and timely as it is a matter being deliberated in several jurisdictions. The consequences or penalties that might apply when a platform is implicated in a counterfeit activity needs to be examined. An approach that allows penalties to be flexible, depending on the specific circumstances might be worth considering. Who should ultimately be responsible for addressing issues concerning defective products sold by third parties on platforms was also discussed, with some arguing that the onus should fall on manufacturers, as is generally the case with traditional retail stores.

Third-party sellers

Verification of the credentials of third-party sellers on platforms is important for platform operators as it is key to building the trust of stakeholders, including consumers and brands. Determining what information should be collected from sellers, the reasonableness of data collection requirements from the perspective of platform operators, and how these requirements compare with those in place for brick-and-mortar establishments deserve attention.

The ability of platforms to authenticate sellers from different jurisdictions may, however, be difficult considering the variability of the "official" documentation that might be supplied by the sellers. The use of fraudulent documentation that counterfeiters would undoubtedly try to use further complicates the matter. A third-party system under which an independent or governmental agency would issue a merchant ID that would be widely accepted could be considered; the impact that this could have on small sellers is, however, a potential concern. Whether such a system would be voluntary, or mandatory was discussed; if voluntary it was felt that there would be pressure over time to make it mandatory. Additionally, such a system would have a negative effect on parallel imports, which under many legislations are legally admissible despite objections highlighted by some rights holders.

Privacy

Platforms are finding ways to ways to exchange information on bad actors, taking into account raising privacy concerns. The results are very promising and need to be continued and, where possible, enhanced. Particular attention needs to be paid to protecting the privacy of parties involved in C2C transactions.

Scope of anti-counterfeiting measures

The limiting of some anti-counterfeiting initiatives to products that endanger health and safety raises several questions, not the least of which is the definition of this class of products. Some argued that a broad definition of health and safety could include well-being, environmental aspects or such fundamental issues as national economic security or human rights (TRACIT, 2019[1]).

Product listings

Platform operators generally provide a great deal of information on the products being sold on their sites and the sellers, distinguishing, where applicable, between products sold by the operator and those sold by third parties. Some have expressed interest in requiring product listings to include a country-of-origin designation. Implementation may, however, be problematic for the platform operators, particularly when it involves the listings by small volume third party sellers, who may not be in good position to accurately designate the country of origin.

Reference

TRACIT (2019), *Mapping the Impact of Illicit Trade on the Sustainable Development Goals,* [1] *Transnational Alliance to Combat Illicit Trade,* https://unctad.org/system/files/non-official-document/DITC2019_TRACIT_IllicitTradeandSDGs_fullreport_en.

3 Frameworks

To succeed, e-commerce platforms need to establish a climate of trust that ensures that sellers are paid, and consumers are provided with a satisfactory product within a reasonable timeframe. In addition, mechanisms need to be in place to resolve disputes between sellers and consumers in a fair and timely manner. Moreover, platforms hosting third party sellers need to ensure that those sellers can be relied on to adhere to the platforms' terms and conditions, which generally includes a commitment to not sell illicit products. The operation of e-commerce, however, has not been left solely to the industry, as it is subject to the laws and regulations promulgated and issued by public authorities, international agreements and targeted actions by governments.

Internet governance

The role that governments should pay in managing the Internet is an ongoing debate, with a rough division into four camps (GCIG, 2016[1]):

- those favouring the continuation of a multistakeholder approach that originated organically from entities forming the technical community;
- those favouring a migration to international institutions based, for example, in the United Nations;
- those favouring a strong governmental model with states exercising sovereign control over their countries' portion of the Internet, accompanied where necessary by international treaties; and, more recently,
- those favouring a multistakeholder approach that involves more conscious deliberation and planning of each stakeholder's respective role.

At the international level, amid concerns that the openness of the Internet was at risk, OECD countries agreed on the desirability of an approach that strengthened international co-operation, while supporting a flexible, multi-stakeholder approach to Internet policy making. This is reflected in a set of 14 principles adopted by the OECD Council in 2011 (OECD, 2011[2]). Furthermore, in 2016, Ministers from 42 OECD and non-OECD countries, and the European Union, adopted a declaration committed to taking a series of actions to promote the development of the Internet (OECD, 2016[3]).

Another relevant international forum to co-ordinate actions to counter abuse of e-commerce in illicit trade in counterfeits is the World Customs Organization (WCO). The WCO Framework of Standards on cross-border e-commerce provides general guidelines, with Standard 9 referring to "Prevention of Fraud and Illicit Trade." Specifically, standard 9 invites customs administrations to "…work with other relevant government agencies to establish procedures for analysis and investigations of illicit cross-border e-commerce activities with a view to prevent and detect fraud, deter the misuse of e-commerce channels and disrupt illicit flow."[1] This general guideline is further complemented by specific implementation tools, including case study examples.

Government-led measures

As discussed below, governments have been active in addressing issues concerning bad actors and e-commerce fraud in recent years, in a variety of ways, by encouraging co-operation with and among stakeholders, and through specific initiatives designed to improve the functioning of e-commerce. In Australia, the government is working on a mechanism through which authorised sellers of branded products could be confirmed by consumers on the seller's website, by clicking on a symbol which links the website to the government's trademark registry, which would authenticate the seller as a supplier of legitimate products. In Belgium, the government has focused on policing the Internet, taking down sites which are trading in counterfeits, in co-operation with law enforcement in other jurisdictions. Considerable attention has been paid to strengthening the registration process for websites; suspicious websites are subject to scrutiny and verification before being authorised.

In the European Union, the United Kingdom and the United States, working groups have been formed to address e-commerce IP issues. In the case of the European Union, a voluntary, non-binding Memorandum of Understanding with rights holders and platforms was created to tackle issues. The EU Commission, which administers the MoU, plays a supportive role that aims to keep the work on track. Participants on the MoU have made commitments in six key areas.

In the United Kingdom, brand owners have been working with the law enforcement to identify websites selling counterfeits. Once claims are vetted, enforcement provides the information on offending websites to the country's web registrar, which organises the suspension of the websites concerned.

In the United States, the government formed an Electronic Commerce Working Group in 2017 to encourage the flow of actionable data and information among major online sales platforms. As part of this initiative, platforms are moving forward with the creation of a private-sector data sharing platform to identify common targets and actionable intelligence about counterfeiters and their criminal networks and will explore opportunities to include additional participants to include shippers, freight forwarders, brokers, social media, and other third-party intermediaries. In January 2020, the US created the Anti-Counterfeiting Consortium to Identify Online Nefarious Actors (ACTION) to monitor adoption and report on the effectiveness of private sector best practices established in the report on *Combatting Trafficking in Counterfeit and Pirated Goods*.

The report identified 10 best practices that platforms and third-party marketplaces could use to enhance their work in this area, and provided for the development of non-binding MoUs with the US IPR Center, which could be used to clarify the expectations and legal understanding for data sharing and coordinated IPR enforcement. ACTION is responsible for monitoring the adoption and efficiency of the voluntary best practices.

Finally, the EUIPO has been working on a webpage providing basic information on the IP protection mechanisms in place at different platforms. As part of the development of its IP Enforcement Portal, it is also developing a system that will enable platform operators to identify brand owner contact points in the different areas of IP infringement. There is also interest in developing a secure system that will allow IP owners to report information on infringement, which could then be accessed by participating platform operators.

Australia

In Australia, a pilot project is underway which seeks to authenticate the merchandise being sold on a platform (OECD, 2021[4]). In 2019, IP Australia, the government agency which is responsible for administering intellectual property (IP) rights and legislation relating to patents, trademarks, designs and plant breeder's rights,[2] developed a Smart Trade Mark mechanism, which is designed to help business and consumers determine whether the products that they are purchasing are authentic (i.e. not counterfeit), using block chain technology. The system enables trademark holders to request IP Australia to attach a business-critical artefact, which in the case of Smart Trade Mark is a URL, to the government's trademark registry. The link can then be verified using Amazon's Quantum Ledger Database (QLDB) service.[3]

The National Rugby League,[4] which has a high level of interest in protecting its brand, has been actively supporting the initiative. In addition to selling merchandise on its own site, the league sells through independent e-commerce sites and the sites operated by its club members. In support of the verification system, a java-script Trust Badge was developed and then deployed in April 2020. When clicked on by users, the badge connects with an API service that reads down into IP Australia's database to see if the e-commerce domain is linked to the trademark. If so, an IP Australia generated confirmation pops up. The system is viewed as helping to boost consumer trust. It is not intended to serve as an enforcement tool, but a future role in enhanced enforcement is not being ruled out. Consumer testing following the introduction of the Trust Badge at NRL-related sites confirmed a statistically significant uptick in trust, particularly at third party retail sites. The badge is currently being used at the official NRL site, 14 club sites and 3 independent retail sites, with plans to expand use to other sites in the future. Feedback from the NRL and club owners has been positive, with club owners looking at how sales were affected following introduction of the Trust Mark.

While there are possibilities to expand use of the Trust Mark to large e-commerce platforms, like Amazon, eBay and Alibaba, the number of vendors operating on such platforms complicates matters and the system would need to be adapted to distinguish between the different vendors. If this could be done, Safe Trade Mark could eventually complement the efforts of the large platforms to fight counterfeiting. In a related area, some trademark holders might be amenable to granting a platform a Trust Mark, while others might be hesitant. In these cases, a mechanism for distinguishing one group from another would need to be developed.

As the programme is being tested, the final cost to the agency and users is yet to be determined, as are the eventual procedures that would apply to rights holders who want to use the system. As matters stand, operation of the system is viewed as relatively inexpensive, even if it results in millions of "hits".

In addition to the NRL Trust Badge Pilot, IP Australia is partnering with the Northern Australia Aboriginal Kakadu Plum Alliance (NAAKPA), the Indigenous Land and Sea Corporation (ILSC) and the Australian Nuclear Science and Technology Organisation (ANSTO) in a Kakadu Plum Pilot, which aims at developing a system of traceability and verification for bush food supply chains, to help ensure these products benefit indigenous communities and enterprises.[5] A trial prototype Smart Trade Mark application has been developed for Kakadu plums. A prototype certification trademark scheme that can be used to denote products that meet "made and grown in Australia" requirements has also been developed, in co-operation with Australian consumer and competition bodies. Eventually the two initiatives could be linked to strengthen supply chain authenticity.

With respect to next steps, efforts are already being made to strengthen co-operation and co-ordination with other government bodies, including customs and border authorities. Outreach to industry has also been pursued, and other trademark holders that are following the project have expressed potential interest in taking part in the system, once it is more fully developed. How unscrupulous operators could be discouraged from counterfeiting the Trust Mark itself would also need to be reviewed to ensure that the consequences of such counterfeiting are sufficient. Introduction of anti-counterfeiting technology in the Trust Mark, in ways that pose ongoing challenges to the counterfeiters, is also being explored and some are ready to be deployed, when needed. To date the system has not been compromised. How the initiative could be expanded to cover platforms outside Australia may also eventually need to be addressed, as would ways to work more closely with foreign jurisdictions which may be interested in developing a similar mechanism. There may also be potential to use the system in ways that would support customs efforts to evaluate the credentials of importers. Also, the idea of adapting and deploying the system across entire supply chains will be reconsidered in the future; the concept was tested early on with several companies, but its complexity suggested that further action should be deferred.

While early in its development, the Smart Trade Mark system has already been recognised with several awards, as follows:

- 2019 AIIA National Winner - Public Sector & Government Innovation
- 2019 AIIA State Winner - Digital CBR Award
- 2019 AIIA State Winner - Public Sector & Government Innovation
- 2019 AIIA State Winner - Infrastructure and Platforms Innovation
- 2019 Blockchain Industry Awards - Government Project of the Year

With respect to further development, the system is designed to be flexible so that, for example, rights holders could eventually explore linking their trademarks with specific product information, with a view towards enhancing their anti-counterfeiting efforts.

European Union

Main governance efforts in the European Union to counter the abuse of e-commerce in trade in counterfeit goods are centred at the European Commission and the EU Agencies, such as the EUIPO. The key initiative is the *Memorandum of Understanding (MoU) on the Sale of Counterfeit Goods on the Internet* facilitated by the European Commission. The EU currently considers two pieces of legislation in the e-commerce area: the Digital Markets Act (DMA) and the Digital Services Act (DSA). Last, the EUIPO administers and implements some specific systems.

Apart from the European Commission and the EU Agencies, EU member states were also taking governance actions to address this risk. An illustrative example are measures taken by Belgium (Box 3.1). Another example is Spain, where Guardia Civil leads Operational Actions (OA) to counter intellectual property (IP) crime; the recent edition of OA focuses on illicit trade of counterfeit automotive spare parts and includes e-commerce as an important component.

Box 3.1. Governance measures in Belgium

In Belgium, counterfeiting levels remain high, but there has been progress in fighting the problem, reflecting the success of the operation In Our Sites (IOS) which was carried out in co-operation with Europol in 2018, with the support of FPS Economy, EURid, DNS Belgium and customs authorities. In 2019 and 2020, some 990 and 1,016 sites, respectively, were shut down. While the number of closures edged upward, it did not match the significant growth in online sales during the pandemic, which is seen as a positive sign.

The Belgian approach has been a proactive one, with increased attention being paid to registration procedures. Until recently, it was relatively simple to set up a domain. After entering basic information, a site would be operational immediately. Once online, applicants would have 14 days to correct any incorrect or fraudulent data, with site closure occurring if no action was taken by the registrant to correct information. With a view towards better protecting consumers and rights holders, EURid and DNS Belgium developed a new screening procedure to identify suspicious sites. Every new domain name is checked against a series of parameters to determine if it is suspicious. If the domain name matches several of the parameters, an 8-step verification process is triggered, which requires applicants to provide proof of identity. Activation of the site is only granted at the conclusion of the verification

---

process. Thousands of suspicious sites are being detected annually, resulting in a significant slowing of the activities of scammers.

The IOS operation has also had a large impact in other economies. Some 21,910 websites were taken down during the operation in the 15 EU member states and 12 non-EU countries taking part in the operation, and counterfeits valued at more than EUR 2.5 million were seized. In addition to Europol, Eurojust played an important role in the operation.

Memorandum of Understanding on the Sale of Counterfeit Goods on the Internet

In 2011, major online platforms and rghts holders for goods for which counterfeit and pirated versions are sold online (e.g. fast-moving consumer goods, consumer electronics, fashion and luxury goods, sports goods, films, software, games and toys) entered into a *Memorandum of Understanding on the Sale of Counterfeit Goods on the Internet* (MoU).[6] The MoU was revised and signed again in 2016, to include key performance indicators (KPIs) that are designed to track its impact and measure its success (EC, 2016[5]).

The purpose of this voluntary agreement is to establish a code of practice in the fight against the sale of counterfeit goods over the Internet and to enhance collaboration between the signatories, focusing on co-operation rather than litigation to achieve results (EC, 2020[6]) and (EC, 2013[7]). The MoU can be considered a 'laboratory'. Reported practices could set a standard for signatory online platforms and rights owners, and may prompt stakeholders not involved in the MoU to perform better in the fight against counterfeiting at national, EU and international level. The agreement is an example of how industry self-regulation can be used to address an important policy issue, with important governmental support. In this case, the European Commission is not a signatory, but it plays a facilitating role, e.g. by organising the meetings and ensuring that all signatories act constructively and in good faith

The agreement is not a legally binding instrument and does not create any contractual or pre-contractual obligations under any law or legal system, nor does it create any liability, rights, waiver of any rights or obligations for any parties or as releasing any parties from their legal obligations. As of 7 October 2021, there were 32 signatories to the MoU, including 15 rights holders, 8 Internet platforms, and 9 industry associations (see Annex II). While the number of participants has increased over time, as discussed below, there have also been few withdrawals (EC, 2020[6]).

The success of the MoU has depended on the following (OECD, 2021[4]) and (EC, 2013[7]):

- A clear incentive for each signatory resulting from the voluntary agreement.
- Safeguards in the agreement to protect the essential interests of each signatory, to cater to different business models and commercial policies, and to ensure legal certainty to overcome resistance within the respective organisations.
- A clearly focused voluntary agreement including well-defined objectives, combined with clearly formulated, realistic obligations, proportionately allocated to parties.
- A high level of consent and commitment within the companies signing up to the agreement.
- Sufficient built-in flexibility to allow for adaptations due to changing circumstances, without having to renegotiate the agreement.
- The presence of an honest broker facilitator (in this case the Commission) to help structure and drive the work and overcome obstacles when difficulties arise.

Key provisions

The revised 2016 MoU is essentially the same as the 2011 MoU, except for the addition of the KPIs mentioned above. It contains a series of commitments by rights holders and Internet platforms to work together to combat online counterfeiting. As shown in Annex I, which provides a summary of some of the key provisions, the commitments are extensive, covering i) notice and takedown procedures, ii) proactive and preventive measures, iii) tackling of repeat infringers, iv) the co-operation, including sharing of information among signatories, v) consumer confidence, information and protection and vi) the supportive role that signatories should play with customs and other law enforcement authorities in their investigations and actions to combat counterfeiting activities.

As indicated, the European Commission plays a key role in managing the agreement, including the organisation of meetings of signatories, which take place as needed, but at least on a biannual basis; in fact, the signatories have agreed to meet twice per year in plenary sessions, and have organised shorter, targeted meetings on topics of interest (such as the Digital Services Act). The Commission is also responsible for preparing an annual report, if needed, on the functioning and application of the MoU. To date, three reports have been issued: a 2013 report on the initial MoU (EC, 2013[7]) and two reports on the 2016 MoU, in 2017 ((EC, 2017[8]) and 2020 (EC, 2020[6]).

Assessment report

The 2020 assessment report reviews the functioning of the agreement, providing i) a general performance review, ii) an examination against three performance indicators, and iii) a summary of the actions taken by signatories under the MoU (EC, 2020[6]). A summary of conclusions and next steps is presented in a final section of the report.

General evaluation of co-operation under the MoU

The report indicates that all signatories agree that the MoU has helped establish or strengthen co-operation. They note that one of the main achievements has been the creation of direct contact points with competent representatives of the signatories.[7] This has made it possible to build trust and ensure quality exchanges, speeding up the receipt of feedback. Some rights owners, however, have highlighted the serious challenges that still need to be addressed. Their views diverge as to the effectiveness of the MoU in terms of its impact on the volume of counterfeits made available online.

Generally, the signatories are satisfied with the practical organisation of the meetings and find that having two plenary meetings a year is sufficient. They consider it useful to invite external experts for the meetings, and appreciate the presentations by technology experts, as new technologies are crucial for staying ahead of counterfeiters.

Most signatories consider the MoU to be "fit for purpose" (i.e. properly designed to meet the objectives of the MoU). However, some rights owners believe that the MoU lacks the efficiency to combat counterfeiting and that the KPIs should be updated. They suggest improving the functioning of the MoU by finding solutions to issues such as repeat infringers and offers of goods for sale that are suspicious, but for which it is difficult to identify IPR infringement. Some rights owners advocate amending the text of the MoU to broaden its scope, by, for example, including other categories of IP infringements besides counterfeiting.

Signatories have made suggestions for topics to be discussed in future meetings. These include infringing listings, multiple accounts, seller anonymity, differentiation between private and commercial sellers, looking at how to enhance data exchanges, and the implications of the platform to business (P2B) regulation,[8] as well as design law cases. Rights owners would also like to discuss the implementation of good practices in more detail.

Most signatories have made suggestions for new actions. These include enhancing tripartite collaboration between online platforms, rights owners and law enforcement authorities, running an information campaign on the MoU at national levels, looking more closely at the retail industry, and including other intermediaries (both online and offline) that are involved in the supply chain. Some signatories have suggested conducting new studies, particularly on online platforms' proactive and preventive measures (PPM) and their treatment of repeat infringers, on technologies used to identify infringing listings and potential counterfeit goods, on sellers' terms and conditions implemented by online platforms to address issues such as blurred/concealed logos and bot-generated seller's contact details.

Support has been expressed for a targeted extension of MoU participation. Rights owners, for example, have expressed interest in including further categories of online intermediaries, such as social media, search engines, payment industry, price comparison sites and websites providing classified advertisements. Online platform operators have also mentioned the payment industry, and shippers and carriers that transport packages as possible areas of interest, as well as expansion of participants to include smaller European online platforms in the MoU.

Key performance indicators

Three key performance indicators (KPI) were established under the 2016 MoU to assist in evaluating the situation with respect to online sales of counterfeits:

- KPI 1: Monitoring the number of offers of alleged counterfeit goods;
- KPI 2: Monitoring the number of listings removed;
- KPI 3: Monitoring the number of seller restrictions imposed.

Monitoring the offers of alleged counterfeit goods is carried out for selected, vulnerable product categories, which are presumably most affected by counterfeiting. The monitored categories include luxury brands (e.g. clothes, shoes, accessories; jewellery and watches), sporting goods (e.g. footwear; football jerseys), fashion brands (e.g. clothes, shoes, accessories; shirts, sweaters, polo shirts), fast-moving consumer goods (e.g. hygiene, cosmetics and personal care products), and electronics (e.g. printers and toners; electronic equipment devices; lighting/bulbs; telecoms equipment, including mobile phones and related accessories; and computers and batteries). With respect to KPI 2, a distinction is made in the reporting between listings that have been removed because of proactive and preventive measures put in place by online platforms, and the number of listings removed because of notifications from rights owners.

Data on the three KPIs for the selected products are collected by MoU signatories every 6 months, for two one-month periods starting on 15 November and 15 May (EC, 2020[6]). The collected data for the three KPIs are then discussed bilaterally between individual online platforms and individual right owners. The agreed results are then sent to the EUIPO, which acts as a trusted party and ensures the confidentiality of individual submissions and a neutral, non-discriminatory evaluation process. The EUIPO then aggregates and analyses the data and then sends them to the Commission and the signatories, and the results are discussed during the MoU plenary meetings.

The data, while illustrative of the situation reportedly have limited statistical value, as:

- KPI data concern only counterfeit versions of selected goods and categories of goods as reported by rights owners;
- the number of listings is limited, and they are only monitored during pre-determined timeframes;
- there is a lack of harmonised methodology and reliable auditing;
- KPI data needs to be considered in the context of the evolving participation of signatories;
- there is no agreement amongst signatories on the interpretation of the data.

With respect to reporting levels, for the six data collection exercises that have been carried out since 2016, data were provided by most rights owners and all online platforms. Some of the rights owners, however, decided not to provide data for some of the data collection exercises, and some of the new signatories were not ready to provide data for the first exercise after their signing of the MoU.

Feedback from signatories indicates general agreement that the monitoring can provide a good overview of trends, but that the mechanism could and should be improved (OECD, 2021[4]) and (EC, 2020[6]). General concerns are that i) data are not collected in a similar fashion and are therefore not comparable,

ii) data sometimes not discussed bilaterally, and iii) there no mechanisms for settling disagreements on the data. These and other concerns were addressed by technical experts representing signatory rights owners and online platforms, in January 2020; ideas on how the process could be improved were exchanged. The experts also highlighted some of the positive aspects of the system, notably:

- the KPIs and data collection exercises provide signatories with a useful and helpful framework to better structure their own monitoring processes;
- the KPIs and data collection exercises provide rights owners with more insight into the visibility of the counterfeit versions of their goods on online platforms;
- bilateral discussions give the opportunity to signatories to raise broader issues, and to rights owners to provide feedback on online platforms' reporting tools.

Practices reported by signatories

The MoU has provided a platform for exchanging information on what participants are doing to address the many challenges that they are facing in combatting counterfeiting. Many of these initiatives or practices are reported in the Commission's reports, which thus serve as an important vehicle for raising awareness of measures that could be taken to strengthen anti-counterfeiting strategies. The 2020 report identifies numerous practices reported by signatories (see Annex III, which contains a summary of reported practices).

Conclusions and next steps

Most signatories assess their collaboration under the MoU positively, indicating that close cooperation and information exchange is key to improving the efficiency and effectiveness of their anti-counterfeiting measures. The signatories appreciate that the MoU is a good platform for exchange, allowing them to discuss the challenges in online counterfeiting in a regular and pragmatic manner. The initiative has also been of significant value to the European Commission in carrying out its work on the fight against counterfeiting.

Some signatories have, however, expressed reservations about its impact. A large group of rights owners has pointed out that many offers of counterfeit goods are still available on the online marketplaces. These signatories consider the cooperation and information exchange with online platforms to fall short of the commitments made under the MoU. Serious concerns have also been raised about the benefits of the KPI data collection exercises. However, both rights owners and platforms supported continuation of the data collection as it provided a useful framework for structuring their online monitoring activities and their bilateral and plenary discussions. In January 2020, three rights owners in the fashion and luxury goods sectors decided to withdraw from the MoU, as they believed that progress was not sufficient, and the level of counterfeit offers was still too high.

More generally, the MoU can be considered a laboratory of sorts, where signatories exchange practical examples of practices on PPM, NTD procedures and ways to share information e.g. on repeat infringers. These reported practices could set a standard for online platforms and rights owners and may prompt stakeholders not involved in the MoU to perform better in the fight against counterfeiting at national, EU and international levels. Signatories encourage other interested parties to join the MoU, in particular traditional e-commerce platforms and classified ads websites. Signatories also recommend that further categories of online intermediaries, such as social media, search engines, payment services, shippers and price comparison portals, be engaged in the MoU process. Ways to involve these stakeholders in at least a limited way are in fact underway.

Signatories have asked the Commission to continue to support their involvement in the MoU initiative, by ensuring that their reported practices are further disseminated, by monitoring their application by online platforms and rights owners, and, if appropriate, by discussing amendments or additions to these practices.

Most signatories agree that at this stage, the focus should not be on revising the text of the MoU. They wish to continue to meet to discuss the KPI results quantitatively and qualitatively, optimise co-operation and monitor the application of good practices. Signatories also wish to discuss new trends, such as design infringements, new fraud patterns, changes in consumer behaviour and, more recently, the consequences of the COVID-19 crisis for the fight against counterfeiting. Interest in examining design infringement reflects the efforts of counterfeiters to avoid traditional anti-counterfeiting mechanisms aimed at trademark infringement. Moreover, targeting counterfeit goods that threaten consumer health and safety, such as electronics, toys, pharmaceutical products and personal protective equipment, could be a crucial next step in the MoU work (EC, 2020[6]). A pilot project to look more closely at goods where authenticity could not be definitively determined has been launched. Finally, there is an interest in delving deeper into certain MoU areas, such as boosting pragmatic ways for online platforms, rights owners and law enforcement authorities to work more intensively together. This is also being pursued as Europol participated in an October MoU meeting, and the EU antifraud office was becoming involved.

With respect to outreach, discussion of the MoU has taken place at World Intellectual Property Organization (WIPO), and with certain non-member countries (notably Colombia and Ecuador), and the EU's experience was shared with Thailand and the Philippines as they developed their own MoUs.

In support of the work on IP, the Commission adopted an intellectual property action plan to support the EU's recovery and resilience in November 2020, which includes provision for the development of a toolbox against counterfeiting, which is designed to improve co-operation among stakeholders and improve data and information sharing (EC, 2020[6]). The toolbox, which is based among others on reported practices and principles developed in the context of various industry-led initiatives, will clarify roles and responsibilities of stakeholders and identify ways to work together. A fundamental element is the sharing of relevant data on products and traders, for which further guidance may be necessary. The toolbox will also promote the use of new technologies such as image recognition, AI and blockchain. Where appropriate, the toolbox will be accompanied by benchmarks to make it possible to measure progress. A roadmap for the toolbox will be published in due course, for comment, and workshops on selected topics are foreseen; it is expected that the toolbox will be published in 2022.

Legislation

Two pieces of legislation are currently being considered by the European Union in the e-commerce area. The *Digital Markets Act* (DMA) aims to ensure contestable and fair markets in the digital sector across the Union where gatekeepers are present. In particular, it aims to address against unfair practices,[9] and practices that could undermine the contestability of markets in the digital sector being carried out by gatekeepers and thereby enhance fair and contestable online platform environment. The *Digital Services Act* (DSA) would establish a common set of rules on intermediaries' obligations and accountability, by i) better protecting consumers and their fundamental rights online, ii) establishing a transparency and accountability framework for online platforms and iii) fostering innovation, growth and competitiveness within the single market.[10]

EUIPO

The EUIPO has been working on a strategic project aimed at enhancing IP protection on e-commerce platforms which involves gathering information about the IP protection programs in place at different platforms, such as eBay, Amazon, Alibaba, Facebook and others. The information is being put on a single webpage to assist IP owners in navigating through the different programs, particularly with respect to the different notification mechanisms.

As part of the development of its IP Enforcement Portal, the agency is also developing a system that will enable platform operators to identify brand owner contact points in the different areas of IP infringement. There is also interest in developing a secure system that will allow IP owners to report information on infringement, which could then be accessed by all platform operators, thereby facilitating and enhancing the effectiveness of the information sharing.

United Kingdom

In the United Kingdom, there is ample evidence that many counterfeit products are being sold on well-known platforms. The problem is significant, even if the overall scope and magnitude of the problem cannot be precisely measured. Information can be obtained from rights holders who are monitoring platforms, consumer complaints and from the platforms themselves, but such information is incomplete; consumer complaints, for example, are likely to be managed bilaterally with no public disclosure, and platforms are similarly likely to address issues with counterfeiting internally, with no public disclosure.

In 2012, the United Kingdom established a strategic objective to make UK domains the safest in the world for consumers and legitimate businesses to trade. Doing so required the UK Government to engage with domain registrars to move against sites selling counterfeits. This resulted in the launching of Project Ashiko where funding was provided to the London Police Intellectual Property Crime Unit (PICPU). Referrals on infringing websites generally selling fake consumer goods are submitted by brand owners, which supply evidence that goods being sold are counterfeit (IP Crime Group, 2020[9]). After due diligence is undertaken by PIPCU, details are sent to Nominet, the UK registrar, which organises the suspension of the infringing domains. The initiative has resulted in 135,000 sites being taken down over seven years. The information that was developed during the operation, when combined with other information, has proved highly useful in improving efforts to remove sites selling counterfeits.

Roundtables were organised with stakeholders to discuss the problems that had surfaced. Raising awareness of the stakeholders of the nature and scope of the illicit activities proved to be of high value of all stakeholders, even if the discussions were often difficult. The platforms developed a keener appreciation of the infiltration of their sites by counterfeits, while rights owners explored ways to interact more effectively with the platforms. The value of brand of protection programmes and possibilities for training were also explored. Eventually the round tables proved useful in developing a shared perspective among stakeholders of what needed to be done to make platforms better for consumers and legitimate business, and difficult for criminals.

A pilot exercise with Alibaba revealed systematic abuse of the platform by counterfeit sellers, paving the way for further investigation and the development of a process for addressing the problem in co-operation with foreign law enforcement authorities. In another exercise, a snapshot of counterfeits on sale on social media platforms revealed 30,000 offers on one day alone, a clear indication of the scope of criminal activities.

It was noted that small companies might not have resources to fight counterfeiting as vigorously as larger entities. The role that platform operators could play in assisting these smaller brand owners was explored in this regard.

The progress made in identifying ways that rights owners and platforms could jointly address problems was seen as having implications for law enforcement, which could then focus resources on platforms which were reluctant to act. Sometimes discussions with the reluctant platforms were sufficient to their taking more forceful actions.

One of the key challenges, however, is dealing with the response of criminals, who have proven to be adept at finding ways around brand protection measures. Some, for example, have sought to undermine IP by replacing brand registration rights recorded by rights holders on platforms, with their records. How this could be stopped expeditiously and effectively will require international co-operation. Attention also needs to be paid to disrupting supply chains, not only at borders but in hotspots, such as warehouses where counterfeits are stored.

How platforms are promoting brand protection was examined in a research project carried out on the take-down procedures employed by different operators. Three distinct approaches were found:

- Platforms with a dedicated platform for referrals by rights holders and a high level of information requirements (major e-commerce platforms were all in this group).
- Platforms with no dedicated platform for referrals and a medium level of information requirements (several social media platforms were in this group).
- Platforms with no dedicated platform for referrals and a minimum of information requirements.

The possible development of a gateway, by government, the private sector or the platforms themselves, to tie the approaches together is seen as being beneficial.

With respect to next steps, efforts should focus on seven points:

- Getting stakeholders to work together to exclude counterfeits by design from being traded.
- Identifying and moving against facilitators and enablers, with particular attention to disrupting money flows.
- Enabling rights holders to use platforms easily.
- Promoting consumer protection and safety on platforms.
- Strengthening international co-operation.
- Enabling safe sharing of intelligence across platforms and with the public sector.
- Hardening systems against current and novel abuse.

United States

The National Intellectual Property Rights Coordination Center (IPR Center) is a US Government body overseen by US Immigration and Customs Enforcement, a part of the US Department of Homeland Security (DHS). The IPR Center co-ordinates the US government's enforcement of intellectual property laws. In late 2017, the IPR Center established an E-Commerce Working Group (ECWG) with major online sales platforms to enhance data sharing among private sector third-party intermediaries involved in e-commerce sales. The effort was intended to test the concept that enhanced data sharing among "competitors" will allow companies to enhance their existing efforts to identify and take down sellers of counterfeit merchandise and provide better target leads to law enforcement for potential criminal investigation. This data exchange pilot has validated the concept that a robust exchange of data is a successful way to identify common targets and actionable intelligence for both the private sector and law enforcement and documented the following:

- Cross-platform illicit activity was found on all rounds of data sharing.
- A review of the combined dataset indicated that the same individual/business used different/multiple IP addresses, business names, business addresses and phone numbers.
- Sellers of counterfeit goods were also targeted in criminal/civil litigation suits for trademark/copyright violations and other illicit activity, to include theft, wire fraud, forgery, cocaine trafficking and money laundering.
- Multiple targets were the subject of HSI intelligence and/or, investigations, or prior CBP seizures.

The project proved to be highly successful, demonstrating the value of a robust exchange of data in i) providing platforms with the information needed to move against bad actors and ii) providing law enforcement information for further investigation and, eventually, interdiction.

In January 2020, the Department of Homeland Security (DHS) published a report on *Combatting Trafficking in Counterfeit and Pirated Goods*, which identifies actions to be taken by departments and agencies to address counterfeiting problems, including development of an Anti-Counterfeiting Consortium to Identify Online Nefarious Actors (ACTION) Plan (Box 3.2) (DHS, 2020[10]).

Box 3.2. Immediate actions to be taken by DHS and recommendations for the US Government to address IP challenges

1. Ensure entities with financial interests in imports bear responsibility.
2. Increase scrutiny of Section 321 environment.
3. Suspend and debar repeat offenders; Act against non-compliant international posts.
4. Apply civil fines, penalties and injunctive actions for violative imported products.
5. Leverage advance electronic data for mail mode.
6. Anti-Counterfeiting Consortium to Identify Online Nefarious Actors (ACTION) Plan.
7. Analyse enforcement resources.
8. Create modernized e-Commerce enforcement framework.
9. Assess contributory trademark infringement liability for platforms.
10. Re-examine the legal framework surrounding non-resident importers.
11. Establish a National Consumer Awareness Campaign.

Source: DHS, 2020.

The ACTION, which builds on the work of the ECWG, comprises the following three elements (DHS, 2020[10]):

- Sharing information within the ACTION framework on sellers, shippers, and other third-party intermediaries involved in trafficking in counterfeit and pirated goods.
- Sharing of risk automation techniques, allowing ACTION members to create and improve on proactive targeting systems that automatically monitor online platform sellers for counterfeits and pirated goods.
- Developing non-binding memoranda of understanding (MoU), with the IPR Center, consistent with US law, to clarify the expectations and legal understanding for data sharing and coordinated IPR enforcement.

Best practices

The ACTION Plan is designed to strengthen information sharing between platforms, while engaging certain other e-commerce entities, including payment processors, shippers and search engines. ACTION would also be used to communicate best practices back to the private sector and monitor, and report on progress and the effectiveness of, these voluntary best practices for the private sector. Ten practices were identified (DHS, 2020[10]):

1. Comprehensive "terms of service" agreements.
2. Significantly enhanced vetting of third-party sellers.
3. Limitations on high-risk products.
4. Efficient notice and takedown procedures.

5. Enhanced post-discovery actions.
6. Indemnity requirements for foreign sellers.
7. Clear transactions through banks that comply with US enforcement requests.
8. Pre-sale identification of third-party sellers.
9. Establish marketplace seller IDs.
10. Clearly identifiable country of origin disclosures.

Comprehensive terms of service agreements

Platforms are called on to conclude stringent terms of service agreements with vendors that provide a legal means to move against sellers of counterfeit goods. Once an infringement is detected, the agreements should allow platforms to impose sanctions such as suspension, termination, and debarment without waiting for a determination by a court. The terms should include escalating capabilities to suspend, terminate, and debar counterfeit traffickers and their affiliates. For major infractions and/or repeat minor infractions, the terms would permit permanent removal of the seller, and any known related seller profiles, from the platform and further result in the forfeiture and destruction of all offending goods in warehouses or fulfilment centres operated by, or under the control of, the platform. The terms should also allow platforms to impose appropriate limitations on products listed, require clearly identifiable country of origin disclosures, impose US banking and indemnity requirements, and significantly improve pre-sale identification of third-party sellers.

Significantly enhanced vetting of third-party sellers

Platforms are called on to develop enhanced vetting, which would encourage platforms to require a seller to provide:

- sufficient identification, including information on its accounts and listings, and its business locations, prior to being allowed to list products on the platform;
- certification as to whether it, or related persons, have been banned or removed from any major e-commerce platforms, or otherwise implicated in selling counterfeit or pirated products online; and
- acknowledgment, where applicable, that it is offering trademarked products for which the seller does not own the rights.

Platforms would then be responsible for vetting sellers, supported by i) use of technological tools and historical and public data, and ii) establishment of an audit program for sellers, concentrating on repeat offenders and those sellers exhibiting higher risk characteristics.

Failure to provide accurate and responsive information should result in a determination to decline the seller account and/or to hold the seller in violation of the platform's terms of service.

Limitations on high-risk products

Platforms are called upon to have protocols and procedures to place limitations on the sale of products that have a higher risk of being counterfeited or pirated and/or pose a higher risk to the public health and safety. In this regard, platforms should prominently publish a list of items that may not be sold on its platforms under any circumstances (prohibited), as well as a list of items that could only be sold when accompanied by independent third-party certification (restricted). In constructing these lists, platforms should consider, among other things, whether a counterfeit version of the underlying product presented increased risks to the health and safety of US residents or the national security of the United States. When a seller claims their merchandise has an independent third-party certification, and this certification is required for the product to be legally offered for sale in the United States, platforms should make good-faith efforts to verify the authenticity of these certifications.

Efficient notice and takedown procedures

Platforms ae called upon to create and maintain clear, precise, and objective criteria that allow for quick and efficient notice and takedowns of infringing seller profiles and product listings. An effective regime should include, at a minimum, the following: i) minimal registration requirements for an interested party to participate in the notice and takedown process; ii) reasonable rules that treat profile owners offering large quantities of goods on C2C platforms as businesses; and iii) transparency to the rights holders as to how complaints will be resolved, along with relevant information on other sales activity by the seller that has been implicated.

Enhanced post-discovery actions

Upon discovery that counterfeit or pirated goods have been sold, platforms are called upon to conduct a series of "post-discovery" actions to remediate the fraud. These should include:

- notification to any buyer(s) likely to have purchased the goods in question with the offer of a full refund;
- notification to implicated rights holders, with details of the infringing goods, and information as to any remaining stock of the counterfeit and pirated goods held in warehouses;
- implementation of practices that result in the removal of counterfeit and pirated goods within the platform's effective control and in a manner that prevents such goods from re-entering the United States, or being diverted to other markets;
- immediate engagement with law enforcement to provide intelligence and to determine further courses of action.

Indemnity requirements for foreign sellers

E-commerce platforms are called upon to require foreign sellers to provide some form of security in cases where a foreign product is sold to a US consumer. Such form of security should be specifically designed to cover the potential types and scope of harm to consumers and rights holders from counterfeit or pirated products.

Clear transactions through banks that comply with US enforcement requests

Platforms are called upon to encourage all sellers to clear transactions only with banks and payment providers that comply with US law enforcement requests for information and laws related to (relevant to) the financing of counterfeit activity.

Pre-sale identification of third-party sellers

Platforms are called upon to significantly improve their pre-sale identification of third-party sellers so that buyers can make informed decisions, potentially factoring in the likelihood of being sold a counterfeit or IPR infringing merchandise. Platforms should implement additional measures to inform consumers, prior to the completion of a transaction, of the identity of storefront owners and/or those responsible for fulfilling a transaction, as well as any allegations of counterfeits being sold by a particular seller. Conversely, if a particular seller is a licensed reseller of the product, this information should also be provided.

Establish marketplace seller IDs

Platforms are called upon to require sellers to provide the names of their underlying business or businesses (if applicable), as well as any other related seller profiles owned or controlled by that seller or that clear transactions through the same merchant account. Platforms could use this seller ID information i) to communicate to the consumer a more holistic view of "who" is selling the goods, allowing consumers to inspect, and consult reviews of, all related seller profiles to determine trustworthiness, ii) to link all related sellers together, which will assist rights holders in monitoring who is selling goods that they believe to be infringing, iii) to better conduct their own internal risk assessment, and make risk mitigation decisions (e.g., requiring cash deposits or insurance), as appropriate, based on the volume and sophistication of the seller.

Clearly identifiable country of origin disclosures

To assist both the platforms and consumers in evaluating the risks that a product might be counterfeit, platforms should require sellers to disclose the country of origin of their products; and platforms should post this country-of-origin information for all the products they sell.

Outcomes, issues and challenges

In December 2020, the IPR Center asked ACTION members to provide written feedback concerning how their existing best practices aligned with any or all best practices outlined in the DHS Report as well as any impediments that complicated implementation. In their responses to the IPR Center and during the expert workshops conducted by the OECD in early 2021, industry partners identified several issues and challenges with respect to the practicalities and effectiveness of some of the voluntary private-sector best practices by parties.

- *Seller vetting.* On some platforms, a significant amount of transactions are C2C and are small volume, which can complicate the thorough vetting of sellers. Not all platforms have the capacity to apply the best practices of human review, technological tools and analyses of historical and public data to assess seller risk.
- *High-risk products.* While the DHS best practices suggested that platforms have in place protocols to limit the sale of "high risk" products. However, there is currently no uniform definition of "high-risk" in this context within the U.S. Government or private sector. Some designate items as "high risk" based on potential health and safety risks (such as counterfeit pharmaceuticals or automotive parts). Others may look at the frequency of sale to determine "high risk" (such as an item with a non-health and safety risks but high-volume sales). A standard definition for high risk would be beneficial to support future investigative/operational issues they participate in.
- *Notice and takedown.* The extent to which current mechanisms in place on platforms work to enable platforms to address quickly the appearance of counterfeit goods on their sites is open to debate.
- *Post discovery actions.* The extent to which the exchange of information between platforms and law enforcement has been taking place in a highly effective manner, enabling law enforcement to identify targets to pursue that go beyond selling on e-commerce sites. Broader information-sharing involving more participants would help combat counterfeiters and disable criminal networks.
- *Indemnity requirements for foreign sellers.* Platforms agree on the importance and value of this requirement. Some have already implemented measures in this regard, while others are exploring ways to do so.
- *Clearing transactions through banks that comply with US enforcement requests.* This is not an issue with those platforms which are already relying on US banks to clear transactions. Other platforms are examining how this could be done.
- *Pre-sale identification of third-party sellers.* Major platforms require sellers to provide their profile details externally, but platforms where C2C transactions predominate have experienced added challenges.
- *Marketplace seller IDs.* Some platforms have already simplified matters by allowing sellers only one profile on their sites This has made it easier for law enforcement to move against bad actors who are operating on multiple platforms.

- *Country of origin disclosures.* Some countries, including the US, require that the country of origin be marked on the product or label. Some platforms see this as a challenging requirement, since they have to rely on vendor declarations.

Overall, the need for all stakeholders involved in e-commerce to co-operate with one another in combatting online sales of counterfeits is great and efforts to ensure this are ongoing. The progress being made on all fronts will be examined in an upcoming report that is expected to be published in the third quarter of 2021.

Legislation

Legislation is currently being considered in the United States to address several e-commerce issues. The *Integrity, Notification, and Fairness in Online Retail Marketplaces for Consumers Act* (INFORM Consumers Act) would require online marketplaces to collect, verify, and disclose certain information from high-volume, third-party sellers.[11] The *Stopping Harmful Offers on Platforms by Screening Against Fakes in E-commerce Act of 2021* (SHOP Act) would, under certain circumstances, hold an electronic commerce platform liable for trademark infringement by a third-party seller of goods where there are health and safety issues.[12]

Industry actions

The major online platforms have developed mechanisms designed to protect customers, brands and their stores from counterfeiters.[13] The mechanisms have focused on several action areas, including:

- *Sellers.* Subjecting sellers to checks prior to their being allowed to trade on the platforms. Sellers are also subject to terms of service agreements that prohibit the sale of counterfeit products and provide the operators with an easy, fast legal basis to act.
- *Consumers.* Providing consumers tools which enable them to determine more easily the identity and particulars of the parties that they are purchasing from.
- *Brand rights holders.* Ensuring rights holders are provided with effective tools to enable them to screen product listings for counterfeits and ensure that these listings are taken down rapidly.
- *Co-operation among the private-sector and with law enforcement.* Platforms and law enforcement are working together to support legal actions against counterfeiters and share intelligence on developments and trends, in a proactive manner. Some are also proactively sharing information on individuals removed from their platform for allegedly selling counterfeit goods as well as intelligence on developments and trends. Platforms are moving forward with the creation of a private-sector data sharing platform to identify common targets and actionable intelligence about counterfeiters and their criminal networks.
- *Development of internal know-how.* Platforms are developing internal expertise to combat counterfeiting and development and deployment of advanced tools that can be used to move against counterfeits in a proactive manner. This includes use of heuristics, algorithms and machine learning.
- *Transparency.* Platforms are expanding their reporting on the results on anti-counterfeiting measures through, for example, annual reports on their activities in this respect.

Sellers

For most platforms efforts with sellers are rooted in comprehensive terms of service agreements that selling partners are obliged to agree to. The agreements, which are non-negotiable, prohibit the sale of counterfeit products and they put sellers on notice of the consequences of doing so, providing the platforms with a clear legal basis to act quickly. Under the agreements, sellers may be required to provide full indemnification for the harm caused by counterfeit goods. Moreover, sellers that reach a specific sales level may be required to carry insurance to cover any damage caused by their products to a US consumer, regardless of where their products are manufactured.

Another example of an effective practice concerns proactive controls on sellers and products. A combination of advanced algorithms, heuristics, machine learning capabilities and investigators are deployed to protect the platform proactively from bad actors and bad products. During registration, for example, sellers may be required to provide a government-issued photo ID and information about their identity, their location, taxpayer information, and a bank account or credit card. Once received, the information can be analysed against hundreds of unique data points to verify the information and to identify potential risk.

A good example of such policy is the know-your-customer (KYC) approach rolled out by eBay, to authenticate sellers on their platform, with a view towards combating all types of fraud. Under the program, prospective sellers need to submit information and "proof of life" evidence that validates their identities, to operate on the platform. The initiative is already yielding positive results. In Brazil, for example, where there was a significant problem with the selling of counterfeit books, use of the KYC mechanism enabled the company to reduce claims from members of the program by 99%.

Walmart applies the verification procedures prior to the sellers' being to operate on the platform. The verification process includes determination of the nature of a seller (i.e. a business or individual), confirmation of its identity, and examination of the seller's online reputation. In addition, vetting is carried out for both high risk products (such as luxury brands, health and wellness items and electronics products) and high-risk geographic regions. The company has expanded its business into fulfilment services, but, based on the experience of others, does not comingle its products with those being shipped on the behalf of other sellers; this is to further insulate its distribution channels from counterfeits.[14]

As bad actors are constantly adapting their operations to evade detection, some platforms innovate to better anticipate the actions of the bad actors. For example, Amazon has established a system of live video verification of identities and documentation. It has proved to be successful, and helped ensure that the people contacted matches the phone numbers they have provided and their photo ID.

Another way that the platforms are seeking to address counterfeiting challenges is through awareness raising. For example, more than 75% of the sellers that were reported by brand owners for selling counterfeit items, or were proactively detected by Mercado Libre, were provided with opportunities to learn about the need to avoid trade in counterfeit products. The purpose of the training is to reach those companies which are unaware of what IP rights are all about. Webinars are run and help is provided on how to avoid posting an infringing item. In addition, brand owners are invited to upload materials that sellers might find useful in identifying counterfeit products.

Consumers

Some actions taken by the platforms are designed for consumers. This includes providing them with additional information about the seller and the product. For example, Amazon offers sellers tools to share more information about themselves and their products. This includes features like profile pages for sellers, store pages for brand owners and an in-house buyer-selling messaging service that allows customers to learn more about sellers and products. Moreover, customers are clearly informed whether they are buying directly from Amazon, or from a third party. In the case of the latter, seller contact information is provided on the product listing; sellers are therefore required to have a single seller ID, which enhances traceability of sales.

Brand owners

Many online platforms provide brand owners with tools to protect against counterfeits. This is, in many cases supported by notice and takedown mechanisms that allow rights owners to efficiently search the platform for infringement and to ensure rapid removal. Information on the reported infringement is used to proactively scan the platform for additional counterfeits.

Another tool are registries of brands, maintained by platforms. For example, Amazon's registry uses heuristics and algorithms and machine learning to predict, prevent and suppress infringement proactively. It captures accurate and actionable information about a brand IP, about their products and about them. Amazon stores prevent infringements using things like keywords and images and product identifiers. Under a program called Project Zero, brands are given an ability to directly remove suspected counterfeit products from the platform, in real time. The information that is generated is again fed into machine learning models and heuristics to help prevent future violations.

Another example is Verified Rights Owner partnership program (VeRO) created by eBay. The program, in which 97,000 rights owners currently participate, provides a mechanism for the rights owners to report on listings that infringe on their copyright, trademark, or other intellectual property rights to eBay, which then takes action to remove the listing. Moreover, the company has dedicated brand protection managers who partner with brand owners to gather intelligence that is then used proactively to detect counterfeit products. Of the 20 million sellers only around 2% have had items removed pursuant to a VeRO notification.

A brand protection program is also maintained by Mercado Libre, under which brand owners can register their full portfolio of IP rights (including trademarks, copyrights, patents and industrial designs). A dedicated web platform is available where the rights owners can provide information on infringements in all the countries in which it operates.

Law enforcement – co-operation

Post-discovery actions include engagement and co-operation with enforcement authorities. It also includes proactive initiatives, where information on bad actors is shared with other e-commerce platforms and other parties. For example, in 2020 Amazon set up an in-house Counterfeit Crimes Unit which is responsible for i) building and referring criminal cases to law enforcement, ii) undertaking independent investigations or joint investigations with brand owners and iii) pursuing civil litigation. This unit, which includes former federal prosecutors, focuses on organized criminal networks and complex financial crimes. The company's efforts have resulted in scores of civil complaints, and several hundred criminal referrals, in the United States, United Kingdom, the European Union, and China.

eBay has also set up a global asset protection team that works closely with law enforcement in support of investigations and the prosecution of cases, and they also assist with training. A new regulatory portal allows participating global regulatory authorities to flag and takedown a listing directly; this is beyond the existing consumer reporting functions on the platform that all stakeholders can already use. The portal is evolving so that authorities will also be able to contact buyers directly in the event, for example, an unsafe product is detected.

Walmart is actively participating in data sharing programs with other marketplaces, with a view towards preventing counterfeiters from moving from one platform to another to maintain their illicit operations.

Internal expertise, in-house capacities

Institutional memory and in-house developed expertise, based on experience from countering counterfeiting are the key foundations for anti-counterfeiting strategies. Several online platforms structure their efforts by creating dedicated teams of highly trained staff to find and detect counterfeits. For example, Amazon invested over USD 700 million and dedicated more than 10,000 employees to stopping fraud, counterfeit, and abuse the teams in 2020. These investments support AI scientists and analysts, an array of detection tools, as well as machine learning and computer vision image detection technologies. Their work is further supported by experts who proactively monitor the platform for items in their field of expertise and report suspicious items to the company; based on their input, items can be delisted automatically, or investigations can be initiated on a priority basis.

At eBay a post-sale authentication program is designed to approach anti-counterfeiting actions in a structured way. The program focuses on specific products, the first of which was watches valued at over USD 2,000. These watches are sent by the seller to a third-party authenticator who is an expert in the field. After authentication the watch is sent to the buyer. If the watch is eventually returned, the returned item is similarly screened by the authenticator prior to being sent back to the seller.

Walmart has procedures that parties can use to report on products that infringe trademarks, copyrights or patents. Moreover, a brands portal was recently launched within which brand partners can report separately on infringements. Once a claim is made on the platform, the company has a policy to immediately block that product, and the company reserves the right to terminate counterfeit seller once the counterfeit offering is confirmed.

Mercado Libre is working in nine discrete areas to combat counterfeiting, including fraud prevention. The investigation department in the fraud prevention team is working closely with law enforcement and other key stakeholders in the public sector to address issues, providing information and other support covering counterfeiting and other types of fraud.

In addition, Mercado Libre is focusing on making the proactive techniques more robust. To this end, the company has recently introduced image brand detector technology, which seeks to undermine the efforts of counterfeiters to avoid key-word detection by analysing the images that sellers put on listings. In some cases, sellers are avoiding the use of any terms that might suggest infringement. The technology will be adapted over time to include an expanding number of brands.

Transparency

Platforms are becoming more open about their efforts to combat counterfeiting. In 2021, for example, eBay released its first ever transparency report, which describes the actions that the company has taken to ensure a safe and trusted user experience on its marketplace, as well as the state of play with respect to listing takedowns (eBay, 2021[11]). Mercado Libre also published its first transparency report in 2021, which provides information on what it is doing to combat counterfeiting, and how the situation is evolving (Mercado Libre, 2021). The report, which covers the period July-December 2020, is set to be updated on a quarterly basis. In addition to IP infringement, the report covers information on other prohibited articles and data privacy. Finally, Amazon detailed its efforts to combat counterfeiting in its first Brand Protection Report, which was published May 2021 (Amazon, 2021[12]). The report reviews how the company has been implementing its three-prong approach, which focuses on i) robust proactive controls, ii) providing powerful tools for brands, and iii) holding counterfeiters accountable.

References

Amazon (2021), *Brand Protection Report*, [12]
https://assets.aboutamazon.com/96/a0/90f229d54c8cba5072b2c4e021f7/amz-brand-report.pdf.

DHS (2020), *Combating Trafficking in Counterfeit and Pirated Goods*, US Department of Homeland Security, Washington, https://www.dhs.gov/sites/default/files/publications/20_0124_plcy_counterfeit-pirated-goods-report_01.pdf. [10]

eBay (2021), *2020 Global Transparency Report*, http://www.ebaymainstreet.com/sites/default/files/2021-05/2020-eBay-Global-Transparency-Report.pdf. [11]

EC (2020), *Report on the functioning of the Memorandum of Understanding on the sale of Counterfeit Goods on the internet, SWD(2020) 166 final/2*, European Commission, Brussels, https://ec.europa.eu/docsroom/documents/42701. [6]

EC (2017), *Overview of the functioning of the Memorandum of Understanding on the sale of counterfeit goods via the internet, SWD(2017) 430 final*, https://ec.europa.eu/docsroom/documents/26602. [8]

EC (2016), *Memorandum of Understanding: 21 June 2016, Ref. Ares(2016)3934515 26/07/2016*, European Commission, Brussels, https://ec.europa.eu/docsroom/documents/43321/attachments/2/translations/en/renditions/native. [5]

EC (2013), *Report from the Commission to the European Parliament and the Council on the Functioning of the Memorandum of Understanding on the Sale of Counterfeit Goods via the Internet, COM(2013), 209 final*, European Commission, Brussels, Ref. Ares(2016). [7]

GCIG (2016), *One Internet*, Centre for International Governance Innovation and Chatham House, http://www.cigionline.org/documents/1045/gcig_final_report_-_with_cover.pdf. [1]

IP Crime Group (2020), *IP Crime and Enforcement Report*, IP Crime Group Secretariat, Concept House, Newport, https://assets.publishing.service.gov.uk/government/uploads/system/uploads/attachment_data/file/913644/ip-crime-report-2019-20.pdf. [9]

OECD (2021), *Discussions with stakeholders*, unpublished. [4]

OECD (2016), *Ministerial Declaration on the Digital Economy*, OECD, http://www.oecd.org/digital/Digital-Economy-Ministerial-Declaration-2016.pdf. [3]

OECD (2011), *OECD Council Recommendation on Principles for Internet Policy Making*, OECD, Paris, https://www.oecd.org/sti/ieconomy/49258588.pdf. [2]

Notes

¹   See WCO e-commerce package, http://www.wcoomd.org/en/topics/facilitation/instrument-and-tools/frameworks-of-standards/ecommerce.aspx

²   See https://www.ipaustralia.gov.au/about-us.

³   See https://docs.aws.amazon.com/qldb/latest/developerguide/what-is.html.

⁴   See https://www.nrl.com/.

⁵   See https://smarttrademark.search.ipaustralia.gov.au/.

⁶   See https://ec.europa.eu/growth/industry/policy/intellectual-property/enforcement/memorandum-understanding-sale-counterfeit-goods-internet_en.

⁷   A list of contact points was drawn up early in the MoU to facilitate communication between the signatories on policy matters related to the MoU as well as to enable direct operational contacts between the brand protection staff of rights owners in different Member States and the sites operated by the Internet platforms (EC, 2013[7]).

⁸   See https://eur-lex.europa.eu/legal-content/EN/TXT/?uri=celex%3A32019R1150.

⁹   See https://ec.europa.eu/info/strategy/priorities-2019-2024/europe-fit-digital-age/digital-markets-act-ensuring-fair-and-open-digital-markets_en#new-rules-in-a-nutshell.

¹⁰   See https://ec.europa.eu/info/strategy/priorities-2019-2024/europe-fit-digital-age/digital-services-act-ensuring-safe-and-accountable-online-environment_en#documents.

¹¹   See www.congress.gov/bill/117th-congress/senate-bill/936.

¹²   See https://www.congress.gov/bill/117th-congress/house-bill/3429.

¹³   Examples in this chapter have been elaborated based on a set of workshops with public and private stakeholders, and on structured interviews with representative of four on-line platforms: Amazon, eBay, Walmart and Mercado Libre.

¹⁴   Fulfilment is a service provided by a platform; it stores and ships products on behalf of its sellers.

4 Conclusions

This report examines the challenges that brand owners, consumers, governments and major online platforms face in the context of online trade in counterfeit and pirated goods, focusing on the latter two. The economic environment surrounding e-commerce is analysed, highlighting the features underlying its large and rapidly evolving role in economies.

One of the keys to the success of e-commerce lies in the efficiencies and conveniences it has introduced into commercial transactions. For businesses, e-commerce has significantly enhanced competition by lowering or eliminating operating barriers, reducing costs, and by vastly expanding the ability of even the smallest businesses to operate globally. For consumers, e-commerce confers benefits by providing information on a much broader range of goods and services that are available on global markets, helping consumers locate sellers and facilitating price comparisons. Convenient delivery options and the possibility for consumers to purchase items easily via computers or mobile devices wherever they are further enhance the attractiveness of e-commerce to consumers, while greatly lowering their search costs.

At the same time, the openness of the Internet and the anonymity that surrounds many online transactions also make it attractive to counterfeiters, providing them with easy access to markets, with low risk of detection and, if caught, relatively low penalties in many jurisdictions. As highlighted by OECD research, in many jurisdictions counterfeiting goes largely unpunished due to difficulties in coordinating effective responses, the impact of corruption in markets, lenient sanctions, and perceptions that these are 'victimless' crimes that do not warrant significant action (OECD, 2018[1]).

The larger online platforms host third-party sellers, which are subject to comprehensive terms of service agreements which are designed to ensure that the sellers operate in ways that establish a climate of trust between the platform operators, consumers and the providers of the goods and services sold on the platforms. The third-party sellers are often individuals or small businesses, about whom little is known. When they operate illegally by, for example, selling counterfeit products, questions arise as to which parties involved in the illegal transactions should bear responsibility when the interests of consumers and brand owners are compromised.

The COVID-19 crisis further exposed the challenges posed by bad actors. During the lockdown, the online environment was misused more intensely, with cyber law enforcement reporting skyrocketing levels of e-crimes. As a result, e-commerce has become a leading platform for trade in illicit products, including fake and substandard medicines, test kits and other COVID-19-related goods.

Quantitative analysis confirms these points. E-commerce is an important vehicle for sales of counterfeit goods, and many types of fakes tend to be ordered online including footwear, clothes, toys, leather goods, electric equipment, watches, cosmetics and automotive spare parts.

Policymakers have recognized the problem and have taken actions to address the challenges, while enforcement agencies have been turning their attention increasingly to the on-line environment. Governments in some jurisdictions have engineered ambitious voluntary agreements with platform operators and other stakeholders that are designed to combat counterfeiting more effectively through enhanced co-operation and collaboration. In addition, new laws are being considered in a number of jurisdictions to deal more forcefully with e-commerce challenges.

Platform operators have also been active in enhancing their efforts to combat sales of counterfeit items. Their efforts are directed at third-party sellers (e.g. by limiting the risk of bad actors selling on a platform), buyers (by providing them detailed information on third-party sellers and through public awareness campaigns) and right owners (by providing mechanisms for monitoring and taking down of IP infringing offerings). In addition, platforms have ongoing efforts to improve their ability use artificial intelligence and machine learning to proactively block attempted abuse of their stores before counterfeiters can even offer products for sale. They have also worked to share information amongst themselves and with law enforcement to identify criminals and purse criminal and civil prosecutions to hold them accountable.

Challenges, however, remain as criminal networks have been able to react quickly and dynamically to avoid detection and circumvent law enforcement. The risk of interdiction, severity of penalties and sanctions applied to trade in illicit products like counterfeits, and the degree to which penalties and sanctions are applied, are factors that parties engaged in such trade take into account when pursuing criminal activities. Simply put, illicit actors will prefer to trade in goods where rewards are highest, and the risks are lowest and the high volume of counterfeiting in e-commerce suggests that national and international legal frameworks, policies, and governance capacities to punish and deter counterfeiting have not yet altered the risk-reward incentive balance for counterfeiters. As a result, governments' and industry response needs to be re-examined and iterated upon regularly. In doing so, important issues need to be addressed, including:

- engaging e-Commerce platform operators in efforts to detect online transactions in illicit products and take action against the criminals and criminal networks behind those illicit activities;
- promoting the establishment of industry-led solutions, including the development of voluntary "codes of conduct" to enable online-marketplaces and other industry intermediaries and sectors to distinguish themselves with standards of excellence;
- the flexibility that platform operators need to respond to emerging threats and the role that industry self-regulation could play in responding to emerging challenges;
- reviewing national and international prioritization of anti-counterfeiting policies and associated resource allocations as well as enabling legal frameworks and the adequacy, and use of, penalties and sanctions to shift the risk-reward ratio for counterfeiters;
- promoting even stronger information sharing and collaboration among government stakeholders, among private-sector stakeholders, and between the private and public sectors to overcome the jurisdictional and institutional gaps exploited by criminals ;
- engaging all intermediaries, to include postal, courier, social media, logistics providers, and payment processors;
- Reviewing the adequacy of information on small shipments and the role of intermediaries and vendors;
- the need for economies to apply the WTO-TRIPS Article 60 *de minimis* exemption only to goods accompanying incoming passengers and not to mail importations and small parcels;
- the need for enhanced scrutiny and vetting of third-party sellers; and
- ensuring the need to adequate protection of the privacy of online stakeholders.

Further analysis is needed to support work in the above areas. In this context, more in-depth country studies would be beneficial, as would efforts to identify and promote best practices.

Reference

OECD (2018), *Governance Frameworks to Counter Illicit Trade*, Illicit Trade, OECD Publishing, Paris, https://dx.doi.org/10.1787/9789264291652-en. [1]

Annex A. Summary of key provisions of the June 2016 EU memorandum of understanding on the Sale of Counterfeit Goods on the Internet

1. **General principles and definitions**
   - General principle
     - ○ The primary responsibility for the protection and enforcement of IPR remains with the respective rights owners and that it is the primary responsibility of Internet platforms to enable a safe online environment for consumers; it is the parties' goal to collaborate in the fight against the sale of counterfeit goods over the Internet.
   - Moratorium on litigation
     - ○ Signatories agreed not to initiate any new litigation against each other concerning matters covered by this MoU, during an initial assessment period of one year.

2. **Notice and takedown procedures (NTD)**

Rights owners should be able to notify platforms about sellers of counterfeit goods, and platforms, in turn, commit to take this information into consideration as part of their pro-active and preventive measures.

   - Reporting procedures
     - ○ Internet Platforms commit to offer efficient and effective NTD, which should be accessible electronically via the websites of the platforms.
     - ○ While notifications may be offer-based, platforms commit to allow notifications to contain multiple offers of the same seller, if such notifications are sufficiently documented.
   - Rights owners' use of NTD systems
     - ○ Rights owners commit to use the NTD offered by platforms for notifications of offers of counterfeit goods and commit to join rights protection programs of platforms (if such programs exist). Rights owners commit to take commercially reasonable and available steps to ensure that they notify platforms of the presence of offers of counterfeit goods, in an efficient and comprehensive manner.
     - ○ In cases where it is obvious that notifications are made without exercising appropriate care, rights owners may be denied or may have only restricted access to NTD.
     - ○ Upon a request by a platform, rights owners commit to pay to the platform the listing fee and the commission fee of any offers that were deleted because of a notification(s) of multiple offers made without exercising appropriate care.
   - Internet platforms' response
     - ○ Internet platforms commit to deal with notifications in an efficient and comprehensive manner, and to take deterrent measures in relation to sellers of counterfeit goods. In cases of doubt, or

where the platform does not have the necessary information to permit the identification of a notified offer, the platform may request additional information from the notifying party.

- Feedback on NTD
  - o Internet platforms and rights owners commit to provide each other with feedback on their notifications. Relevant sellers should also be informed where an offer has been taken down, including the underlying reason, and should be provided with the means to respond.

3.   **Pro-active and preventive measures**

- Measures by rights owners
  - o Rights owners commit to take steps to effectively fight counterfeiting at its source and to actively monitor platforms with the aim of identifying and notifying offers of counterfeit goods to platforms.
  - o Rights owners commit to take steps to provide and update general information to Internet on specific products that present substantial and pervasive counterfeiting problems on platforms.
  - o Rights Owners commit to provide to platforms at their request a list of keywords commonly used by sellers for the purpose of offering for sale counterfeit goods and to assist platforms, as appropriate, with their proactive and preventive measures.
- Measures by Internet platforms
  - o Platforms commit to take steps to request seller contact information and to verify this information.
  - o In pursuing their pro-active and preventive measures, platforms commit to take into consideration information provided by rights owners that is not exclusively related to specific offers.
  - o Platforms commit to take measures to identify and/or prevent pro-actively the sale of counterfeit goods, and to prevent such goods being offered or sold through their services.

4.   **Co-operation, including sharing of information**

- By Internet platforms
  - o Platforms commit to adopt, publish and enforce IPR policies.
  - o To facilitate legal actions and investigations into the sale of counterfeit goods, platforms commit to disclose, upon request and where possible, relevant information on alleged infringers.
- By rights owners
  - o To, or in connection with, legal proceedings or investigations, rights owners' requests for the disclosure of the identity and contact details of alleged infringers should be made in good faith.

5.   **Consumer confidence, information and protection**

- o Internet platforms and rights owners commit to provide appropriate means to consumers to identify and report offers of counterfeit goods, prior to, or after purchase, to platforms and to rights owners.
- o Platforms commit to assist consumers who unintentionally purchase counterfeit goods on their websites.

6. **Repeat infringers**

- Internet platforms' policies

  - Internet platforms and rights owners commit to cooperate in the detection of repeat infringers.

  - Internet platforms commit to implement and enforce deterrent repeat infringer policies. These policies should include the temporary or permanent suspension or restriction of accounts or sellers. Platforms commit to use their best efforts to prevent re-registration of permanently suspended sellers.

  - Platforms commit to share, upon request and where possible, information on suspension of repeat infringers on an individual and case-by-case basis with the rights owners concerned.

- Rights owners' monitoring

  - Rights owners commit, where possible, to provide information to platforms concerning those sellers they believe to be repeat infringers and commit to provide feedback to platforms on the effectiveness of platforms' policies regarding repeat infringers.

7. **Co-operation with customs, border authorities and law enforcement authorities**

  - Rights owners and platforms commit to cooperate and assist law enforcement authorities, in the investigation of the sale of counterfeit goods.

8. **Assessment and follow-up**

- Assessment period

  - The MoU was subject to an initial assessment period of twelve months, during which the signatories were to meet quarterly under the auspices of the European Commission, to analyse the progress, implementation and functioning of this MoU based on agreed Key Performance Indicators (KPIs).

  - The signatories, together with the European Commission, were to meet at the end of the assessment period to evaluate, based on a report prepared by the European Commission upon consultation of the signatories, the effectiveness of the MoU, to discuss the continuation of the MoU and, if appropriate, to discuss and propose appropriate follow-up actions.

- Review

  - After the initial assessment period, signatories would consider prolonging the MoU for an indefinite period.

  - Each year, the European Commission would consider preparing a report, in consultation of the signatories, on the functioning and application of this MoU.

  - The signatories of the MoU were to meet, under the auspices of the European Commission, biannually or more frequently if serious problems arose, to i) consider the functioning or the application of the MoU, ii) review the MoU and iii) take further steps, if necessary.

- Signatories

  - Each signatory may at any time terminate its participation in the MoU by notification to the other signatories and the European Commission.

  - Each signatory may at any time request the European Commission to convene a plenary meeting of all or specific signatories, if it feels that a signatory is not respecting the principles established by this MoU. Signatories, after consultation with the European Commission, may decide to ask such a signatory to withdraw from the MoU.

Annex B. **Signatories to the June 2016 EU Memorandum of understanding on the Sale of Counterfeit Goods on the Internet, as of 28 April 2021**

Rights owners

- Adidas International Marketing BV
- Apple
- Duracell
- Hermès
- Lexmark
- Luxottica Group Spa
- Moncler Spa
- Nike Inc.
- Philip Morris International
- Philipp Plein
- Procter & Gamble
- Royal Philips
- Signify
- Zanellato

Online platforms

- Alibaba Group Inc.
- Amazon Services Europe Sarl.
- bol.com
- eBay
- Facebook Marketplace
- Grupa Allegro sp. z o.o.
- OLX
- Rakuten France

Business associations

- Anti-Counterfeiting Group (ACG)
- AIM European Brands Association
- Business Action to Stop Counterfeiting and Piracy (BASCAP)

- European Federation of Pharmaceutical Industries and Associations (EFPIA)
- Federation of the European Sporting Goods Industry (FESI)
- International Video Federation (IVF)
- Motion Picture Association (MPA)
- Toy Industries of Europe (TIE)

Source: EC, 2021.

Annex C. **EU practices to combat the online sale of counterfeit goods**

(Extracts from EC, 2020b)

I. Proactive and preventive measures

Fighting counterfeiting at its source

Rights owners report fighting counterfeiting at its source as a top priority, with the focus on tracing manufacturing facilities, supply routes and criminal networks, thereby facilitating law enforcement efforts to seize counterfeit goods and shut down factories and warehouses involved in manufacturing and distributing them.

Most rights owners and online platforms have set up dedicated internal teams responsible for IPR enforcement globally. These teams work with law enforcement authorities, including customs authorities. In key jurisdictions, rights owners are providing up-to-date descriptions, photos and samples of their goods, and training to facilitate the identification of counterfeit goods. They are also working with law enforcement authorities to investigate and take down international counterfeit distribution networks.

Providing product information and keywords

Rights owners report that they are providing online platforms with training and/or training materials, guidelines and tips facilitating the identification of counterfeit goods and permitting the recognition of high-risk sellers. They have also contributed to awareness-raising events and inform online platforms, where appropriate, of i) new product releases, to alert them to goods that are particularly susceptible to being counterfeited, ii) goods that are not manufactured by a specific brand, iii) keywords used by sellers to refer to counterfeit goods and iv) the latest trends. Online platforms confirm the value of these initiatives, while expressing interest in more active involvement of a larger number of rights owners.

Seller's identity verification

Online platforms indicated that they have several processes in place to vet sellers and identify bad actors, to ensure they do not negatively affect the experience of customers. These checks are usually carried out when a new seller applies to open an account, and, depending on the platform in question, may include examination of identity documents as well as payment instrument verification. Online platforms have developed various proprietary systems to analyse hundreds of unique data points gathered by the online platforms, to identify potential bad actors.

Rights owners are also monitoring online marketplaces to identify actors offering counterfeit goods. While some rights owners have set up monitoring teams in their IPR enforcement or brand protection departments, others outsource monitoring online websites to specialised consultants. Rights owners also work closely with anti-counterfeiting associations and payment processors, and work on developing new technologies to help identify counterfeits. In that context, rights owners have indicated the usefulness of enabling automatic scanning using a search and enforcement application programming interface (API).

Proactive identification of offers of counterfeit goods

Online platforms report that they are continuously developing policies and tools that make it possible to verify offers before publishing them on the online marketplaces they manage. The online platforms started working on those policies and tools before joining the MoU, but in some cases, their involvement in MoU-related work has facilitated the roll-out of measures proactively identifying offers of counterfeit goods. Their efforts rely on input from rights owners and feedback from consumers.

Rights owners acknowledge that many online platforms use automatic filters to identify offers of counterfeit goods, but believe that such filters should explore the possibility of including keyword-based filters and image-based filters (to detect digital fingerprinting embedded in images of goods, blurred logos, QR codes, etc.). Rights owners have proposed a list of indicators they use in their own enforcement efforts and which they believe should also be considered part of PPM by platforms:

Brand protection programmes

Most online platforms which are MoU signatories have created specific brand protection programmes. Brands that decide to participate in brand protection programmes with platforms gain access to tools such as upgraded and/or simplified notice and take-down (NTD) procedures, dashboards with additional feedback on the follow-up given to the notification, or integrated search tools facilitating the identification of listings infringing IPR using text-based and image recognition. The IPR violations reported through such programmes are used by online platforms to train their machine-learning algorithms, which then use the information provided to boost their PPMs. At least one online platform has launched a brand protection programme that gives rights owners access to a self-service tool permitting the immediate takedown of goods violating trademark rights.

II.   Notice and take-down (NTD) procedures

Experience with NTD procedures

Rights owners confirm the value of NTD procedures and are eager to see them further developed to enhance their effectiveness and simplify their use. Online platforms, which reportedly invest heavily in developing NTD procedures, agree that cooperation under the MoU has had a positive impact on their work on NTD procedures. Cooperation with and feedback from the rights owners, and the exchange of ideas and experiences with other marketplaces, have helped them improve existing processes, and in some cases introduce new functionalities.

The concept of "trusted flaggers"

In response to an EC recommendation on tackling illegal content online, platforms have established special notification channels for "trusted flaggers", which are governmental entities with specific expertise in identifying illegal content online. The flaggers include customs, police and market surveillance authorities, consumer protection authorities, competition authorities, any other enforcement authorities and administrative authorities.

Reacting to notices

In the context of the MoU, online platforms have undertaken a voluntary commitment to assess the completeness and validity of notifications, and deal with notifications in an efficient and comprehensive manner, without undue delay. They have also committed to ensuring that valid notifications of offers of counterfeit goods lead to a swift removal or disabling of the notified offer, and to take deterrent measures in relation to sellers that have placed such an offer. Moreover, relevant sellers are to be informed when an offer has been taken down, including the reason, and should be provided with the means to respond.

III. Repeat infringers

Identification of repeat infringers

Online platforms are using proprietary systems to analyse data of every new user who wants to register as a seller at their marketplace. The systems analyse various unique data points and user information to identify potential counterfeit or other infringement risks, including verifying whether the account could be related to another account previously removed from a given platform. Such monitoring systems are based on various risk indicators depending on the platform, including, but not limited to, data provided through NTD procedures by users and rights owners. They also incorporate automatic filters to prevent the re-appearance of the same content, and make it possible to examine all accounts linked to a specific user. The platforms also rely on information provided by rights holders to complement their efforts in this area. While considerable progress has been made in addressing issues concerning repeat infringers, it has been flagged as an area where further co-operation is needed.

Repeat infringer policies and sanctions

Online platforms are using graduated measures restricting a seller's activity on their service to deter those who offered counterfeit goods in the past from continuing to do so. These measures include, depending on the platform, warnings, temporary account restrictions, temporary account blockage, and permanent account blockage. Once the seller is permanently blocked, re-registration is forbidden. Some platforms, under specific circumstances, would withhold payments for goods confirmed to be counterfeit. Applying these measures has a direct impact on a seller's rating and their possibility of becoming a recognised/certified seller.

IV. Cooperation, including sharing information

Setting out clear policies

All online platforms report that they have developed clear rules on protection and enforcement of IPR on the websites they operate. Some provide users with additional documents such as anti-counterfeit policy or specific guidelines for sellers.

During discussions during the MoU meetings, signatories indicated the following key elements for robust seller account policies:

- a clear indication that only genuine goods can be sold and the sale of goods infringing IPR is forbidden, and will lead to a sanction of the seller;
- clear requirements on providing correct information about the goods offered;
- an explanation of the PPM used, the NTD procedures, and policies against repeat infringers, including sanctions that can be applied, so sellers are aware that their listing may be removed and their accounts blocked;

- a requirement to use authorised pictures that sellers are authorised to use, and to use pictures of the actual goods offered.

Transparency

While the MoU did not set out commitments on publishing transparency reports showing the effectiveness of the measures the signatories put in place, many stakeholders do so, either as part of a public consultation launched by the Commission or in their publicly available transparency reports.

Facilitating legal actions

Under the MoU, the signatories have committed themselves to exchanging information to facilitate legal proceedings and investigations into the sale of counterfeit goods. To this end, platforms have undertaken to cooperate with rights owners in accordance with the applicable laws, and, to disclose, upon request, relevant information. This includes the identity and contact details of alleged infringers and their usernames, as permitted by applicable data protection laws. Rights owners have undertaken to submit disclosure requests in good faith and in compliance with applicable law, including data protection laws.

Improved information exchange

Signatories agree that one of the main achievements of the MoU has been the creation of direct contact points with competent representatives of the signatories. This made it possible to build trust and ensure quality exchanges, speeding up the receipt of feedback.

V.   Co-operation with customs and other law enforcement authorities

Rights owners and online platforms both reported that they regularly co-operate with law enforcement authorities. They do so in particular by launching proceedings against individual infringers, and by assisting law enforcement authorities in their own investigations. The signatories said that they cooperate both with the European authorities and authorities in third countries (mostly in Asia) to address the problem of counterfeiting at its source.

Some online platforms reported that they had put in place dedicated internal teams and processes to cooperate with law enforcement authorities and meet their information needs.

Many of the rights owners have long-standing specific programmes in place to cooperate with customs, police and other law enforcement authorities to detect and investigate the sale of counterfeit goods and prosecute counterfeiters. They often assist these authorities as experts on the authenticity of the goods, answering queries, providing expert reports, and sending experts directly on site to support the authorities' actions.

Rights owners regularly meet with law enforcement authorities, participate in enforcement operations, and launch criminal proceedings jointly with the authorities. Many of them organise training sessions for customs and other law enforcement authorities, to make it easier for them to recognise counterfeit versions of their goods.

Many rights owners are users of the IP Enforcement Portal managed by the EUIPO. The IP Enforcement Portal enables rights owners to:

- securely share information on their IPRs with law enforcement authorities, along with contact information and product details, production and logistics;
- send alerts to law enforcement authorities;

- help law enforcement authorities to recognise counterfeit goods and act, including by helping the authorities to quickly verify suspicious cases;
- streamline the process of filing an application for action, by offering a translation module.

Both rights owners and online platforms have suggested inviting representatives of law enforcement authorities to the MoU meetings, to start a discussion of how the signatories can support those authorities in their anti-counterfeiting actions in a more effective manner.

VI.   Consumer confidence, information and protection

All platforms make it possible for consumers to report violations of IPR, with the help of dedicated notification tools. All of them allow consumers to approach the sellers directly to obtain confirmation of goods' authenticity or other qualities, and make available product reviews and seller ratings, based on user feedback and selling history. They assist consumers who have unintentionally purchased counterfeit goods in obtaining compensation, by either directly refunding the purchase or by initiating a refund procedure with the seller. Some platforms have put in place special protection programmes for buyers.

Rights owners report that they are also approached by consumers who have questions on the authenticity of goods purchased online. They answer such questions both through dedicated tools to report counterfeits and through general customer service. In addition, some of them have put in place training programmes for their retail staff on how to answer the queries of customers reporting suspicious goods. Many rights owners use authentication systems (e.g. codes, labels) that allow consumers to verify the authenticity of the goods directly. Rights owners actively participate in various campaigns to raise consumers' awareness of risks related to purchasing counterfeits.